CREATIVITY IS...

WHATEVER YOU WANT IT TO BE!

ADRIANA MONIQUE ALVAREZ   REGYNA CURTIS

RENÉ DEANDA   MICHELLE LEE DESIMONE

GRACE EKALL   NICOLE GARRITANO, DNP

SUSAN J GROSS   NICOLETTE HALLADAY

DIANE HAZELWOOD   PAUL HEMSTREET

MUHNOO SOPHIA JAIN   DANETTE KUBANDA

MAYRA LEEN   EMILY NORTHEN   DAWN PHOENIX

ATOUSA RAISSYAN   ELIZABETH SOSNER

DR. KRISTINA TICKLER WELSOME

WENDY VIGDOR-HESS   LAURA GARCIA

Express Yourself
PUBLISHING

CONTENTS

INTRODUCTION

Have you always thought that to be "creative" you have to be good at drawing or painting? Many have taken on this definition and believe it as truth. These twenty amazing contributors are all here to expand the "societal" definition of creativity beyond a pencil and a paintbrush.

Having interviewed hundreds of people I have come to realize that people have defined creativity in such expansive ways! It is so exciting to hear it described as; discovering their own magic and owning it, thought moving into action and birthing potential into reality, just to name a few. These definitions and perspectives really get at a person's true essence, basically all that we are and want to be.

My wish is for you to be inspired by these stories and to feel included and empowered. I want you to notice your own strengths, perceived weaknesses and create your own definition of creativity so you can feel more joy, love and happiness. It is that simple, yet we make it that complicated.

We are the creators of our own life making choices every moment. Join us in being active participants in this thing called life to embrace and own your creative expression and talents that make YOU, YOU.

Creatively yours,
Hollis Citron

ADRIANA MONIQUE ALVAREZ

CREATIVITY IS THE ACT OF CREATION

*L*ike most kids growing up I didn't see myself as creative. I wasn't particularly good at drawing or painting. The art teacher never saw anything special in me and as a result I didn't consider myself artsy. I thought creativity was like blue eyes, some people get it and some people don't.

What I learned after I left the school system is that every single person on the planet is creative. Creativity actually doesn't have much to do with art and has everything to do with the ability to **create.**

Once I saw it through this lens I knew I that I was not only creative, but a powerful Creatrix.

This shifted the way I moved through life. At 21 years oldI was living in Albania as a volunteer in a state run orphanage. I read the book Success Principles by Jack Canfield and I remember for the first time realizing that I had the power to create my life. And my success in life was not based on if I want to college or not, if I got good grades, if I married a wealthy man or got a good job. My success was based on my ability to intentionally create what I desired.

I quickly learned that the difference between those who are intentional and those who aren't comes down to connection. The more I was connected to myself, my heart, my purpose for being here the better it felt. In addition to this, the more I strengthened my connection to God, Source, all of life that supports me the more powerful I felt. From this place of connection my thoughts, visions, and actions began to feel more true to me.

I began to connect the dots between those three key components.

Thoughts, visualization, and action.

This is how I began to create. I practiced focusing my conversations on what I desired, what felt good and expansive. I would imagine what I desired and I would experience it like it was already real and then my actions naturally fell in line with the first two.

Living thousands of miles from home gave me the space to experiment and practice this with minimal input from others. I had to get to know myself. Who was I outside of my family, outside of my country, and outside the expectations and plans of others? Without answering these questions I couldn't figure out what I desired.

It took me about ten years to fully become myself. To know that I what I was wanting was my desire and not the desire of someone close to me. In this time I shed and mourned the need to be liked by others. The urge to please others and I began to tune into what made me incredibly joyful and light.

It was still delicate though and when I visited home or got too close to the input of others I could feel my core and foundation rumble and shake.

I continued to practice and used this art of creation to meet my husband, to start a successful business during a recession, and to have children after being told it was in the cards.

Over the last couple of years I have felt my creativity shift.

I began to crave even more joy, more lightness, my effortlessness.

It felt a little greedy. I explored how good I am allowed to feel. How much fun adults are allowed to have. How easy can it be to make money and still be ethical. And a big one, how long do I have to grief and be brokenhearted after the loss of a child.

This journey was a deep one and it confronted everything I was taught. Every value that was instilled in me. Every cultural norm-it all came into question.

One of the most challenging aspects for me was that it felt a little disrespectful. Was it ok to find a different way, maybe even a better way than my grandparents of parents had found? Was it acceptable to not work hard? To not worry about bills? To take any random Tuesday off to swim in the river with my boys? What if the actions I was now considering weren't the actions that traditionally lead to a desired outcome?

What if making boba tea in my kitchen was the action that lead to me knowing what I wanted to do next in my business?

What if having a dance party in the living room was what lead to having clarity on an idea?

It didn't feel strategic or responsible, but it felt GOOD.

I remember walking down Magazine Street in New Orleans on a balmy moming and I heard the words, how much pleasure can you take without guilt?

What?

How much pleasure can you allow yourself without feeling guilty?

How good can your life feel without you feeling a twinge of shame?

How brightly can you shine without apology?

Oh I could feel my throat close and my chest tighten.

I had already hit the point in my life and business where I was moderating what I shared because if people knew what it was really like, they would hate me.

It was that week that I started having weekly massages and it felt sinful. Once a month, fine. Once a quarter, great. Weekly? Who do you think you are?

I would walk to my favorite spa and set the intention of enjoying every minute of it and it wasn't as difficult as I thought it would be. I would leave feeling like I was walking on clouds and every single time I would have an idea pop in that felt so incredibly fun and easy. I would act on the idea and boom, good things would happen.

I continued practicing this with a variety of things including how many hours I worked or how much time I took off. How often I went to my favorite restaurant. Turned out I had quite a high threshold for pleasure and guilt was no where to be found.

The next two were where I had my biggest struggles or maybe more accurately where I had more to unlearn.

Since having a full term stillbirth I had sentenced myself to a lifetime of "you must feel bad about what happened". I intellectually knew it wasn't my fault, but I couldn't believe it with all of me. If I went a week or two without thinking about my daughter and what happened I would feel ashamed. It became the cloak I required myself to wear like the women in Albania who wear black after their husbands pass.

It took me two years to let the shame go and for me to open my cell and walk out of that prison. Interestingly enough it fully clicked while I was on a live interview about motherhood. I was feeling particularly light and gave the woman permission to ask me about anything, including Nina.

All of a sudden I could feel myself floating above my chair, everything faded, and I slowly said the words. I buried a child and what if there's nothing wrong with that? It clicked-it all finally clicked! What if it happened and I didn't have to punish myself for life? What if I didn't have to be sad or mentally rehash it again? What if it served a beautiful purpose and it didn't have to be heavy and I didn't have to mourn anymore?

That night in my meditation I saw a circle of women in my yard leaping six, eight, ten feet into the air celebrating my liberation.

I knew I was accessing even more of my creative juices.

Recently I was telling a friend how much I am enjoying writing, cooking, and playing with the boys. She lovingly replied, you are absolutely glowing! I realized that when I am creating a beautiful life I have the glow that we often associate with pregnancy. Holding and cultivating life in my body felt like the truest expression of me. The amazing thing is that I can recreate it every single day.

Last year we moved to where I am from in rural Colorado and creation moved into full swing. We planted loads of new trees, put dozens of plants inside and out, flowers and herbs everywhere.

Our property was full of life and beauty and I was feeling the same way being connected to it.

I was organizing Sunday family dinners, having holiday parties, and sharing this energy with those closest to me. One day it all came crashing down when my brother expressed his anger about us moving home. He did not appreciate my glow and saw it as arrogant. He declared that my boys couldn't be around his daughter and instantly broke their hearts.

For nine months there has been conflict and ultimatums.

The underlying theme and trepidation has been if you just tone it down and dim your light you probably wouldn't have caused this. Finding and celebrating myself thousands of miles of home was one thing, being the fullest and most authentic me with my family at my house every week was a whole new thing.

They weren't on that journey with me. They don't know who I am as an adult. They don't actually know what my soul's work is or what I do in the world.

I have been silently sitting with this. Looking myself in the mirror and asking if I am willing to be someone else that fits better in my family and hometown. Can I be a little more of a doormat and a little less outspoken? Have I been on a twenty-five year journey only to renounce myself and revert back to people pleasing?

I have been given the idea to write books and start a podcast with my boys highlighting the little moments that lead to them saying, THIS IS THE BEST DAY EVER!

But I can't speak and write more and simultaneously dim my light or shrink in the presence of my family

This morning I laid in the early morning silence and with tears streaming down my face, I chose to honor myself. No one else has to understand it or agree with it, but I must be true to myself.

I will not be intimidated into being anything other than myself.

This is creativity.

Honoring all that we are.

Creativity is denying none of our power or potential.

Creativity is accessing the parts of us no one could see or believe in

Creativity is creating the life we came here to live, without apology.

What I never knew as a little girl was that I could live a big life or do something important.

I thought the meaning of life was to be a chameleon, conforming to what others wish. Taking up as little as space as possible. Mastering how to be polite and nice. *Always* put others first and hoping for the best.

What I discovered was that life is whatever we want it to be. We hold the wand. We do not need permission from anyone, but ourselves. And our lives expand with courage and belief.

This quote is painted on the wall of my favorite coffee shop, "At any given moment, you have the power to say, this is not how my story will end."

It serves as a constant reminder that life is not static. We hold the power. We are the creator of **our days.**

Wherever you are on the journey, my prayer is that you will remember who you are, that you will feel the support that is all around you, and that you will know the thoughts you think, the future you imagine, and the actions you take are the way to everything you imagined and more!

May *y*ou walk in beauty and honor your Soul.

You were born for such a time as this.

You are a powerful Creator!

ABOUT THE AUTHOR

ADRIANA MONIQUE ALVAREZ

Imagine a world without gatekeepers and censorship. This is what inspired Adriana Monique Alvarez to start AMA Publishing and train a global network of female owned publishing houses. She's a USA Today bestselling author and has been seen in Forbes, Entrepreneur, Huffington Post, International Living, America Daily Post, London Daily Post, and Grit Daily.

She is currently living in the middle of nowhere Colorado where she is renovating her grandparents home and learning how to homestead with her husband Derek, and two sons, Sam and Grant.

Website: https://adrianamoniquealvarez.com/

REGYNA CURTIS

ANSWERING THE WHISPER AND FINDING MY SOUL WISDOM

*C*reativity is the process of birthing potential into reality.

In other words, creativity is life. We are often too busy with life, though, to pay much attention to our creativity, especially as adults. This was the case for me for many years, yet as I look back now, I can identify the whispers from my soul that continuously reminded me to come back into the space of my creativity over and over again. Until one day, I decided to engage in the conversation.

"You need to create something" I heard the whisper say.

"Create what?" I asked.

ACKNOWLEDGING THE WHISPER

In early 2020, the world came to a screeching halt in what felt like an instant. The reality I had known for years—sleeping in hotels more than my own bed, constant flights, and travel, always on the move— suddenly and completely stopped. I began canceling flights and moving in-person meetings to Teams. My beloved yoga classes moved to Zoom calls, and I suddenly found myself spending day upon day in my home office surrounded by my art supplies. **I could hear them calling to me.**

On the wall facing my desk is a map of the world, bordered by photographs that I have taken on my adventures. The **rainy grey** hills of China shot through an opening in one of the many shelters that pop up along the Great Wall, the **greenest** valley I've ever seen in New Zealand, the **icy blues** of Gulfoss waterfall in Iceland, **purple and chartreuse** Chihuly glass reflecting off of a pond of lily pads in the gardens at the Biltmore in Asheville. Snapshots, taken to help me remember these moments; not just the moments, though, the **colors.**

I've always seen the world through colors. **I remember and understand the world through the language of color.** I vividly remember the colors and the textures of the clothing worn by myself and others from some of the most poignant moments in my life. Color shows me the way, helps me remember, and heals me. Looking at the photographs on my office wall, I can instantly transport myself to the moment when I took them. I can feel the air around me, know who I was with, and even smell or hear that particular location as if I were standing there again.

I now know that **this relationship with color is one of the languages my soul wisdom uses to communicate with me.**

Long before I could identify art as a part of my soul language, I heard a whisper in my heart that led to me enrolling in college as an art student. Eventually, I landed in art education classes, and not long after, my professional story began as an art teacher. To be honest, it started well before that as an entrepreneur, artist, teacher, and intuitive being, but for the purposes of the professional training for what we collectively call a career, it began as an art teacher.

For as long as I can remember, there has been a whisper in my heart guiding me, "... *there's something more.*" This whisper led me on a winding path through the worlds of higher education and educational travel before landing me in a level one Reiki class as a birthday gift to myself on my 37th birthday. This was the moment when **I actually started to listen to what this whisper was telling me.**

ENGAGING IN CONVERSATION

A few years earlier, I found myself sitting in bed on a Saturday morning in an Airbnb in Melbourne, Australia. I was living there for a few months for work. For the seven years before that moment, I had traveled somewhere approximately every two weeks. I hadn't spent more than a few weeks in any one location, including my home; wherever that was at the moment. It was Philadelphia, but it was hard to call it home because I had hardly been there.

I had been in Melbourne now for almost two months, and while during this time I had traveled to China and Kangaroo Island, and this was now my third residence in Melbourne, I felt more settled than I had in years. How interesting that I'd managed to create daily routines here, which I couldn't seem to incorporate while in my home city. I had found a favorite yoga studio, I took the tram to work each workday, devoured several audiobooks along the daily commute, and had favorite cafes to visit on the weekends for some of the best lattes and avocado toast I'd ever tasted.

On this particular morning, as I sat in the silence of the day preparing for my lackadaisical stroll to an alley café nearby and dreamed of which far corner of the city I would explore, I heard the whisper say something different:

"You need to create something," it said. And because I had nothing more important to do and nowhere I needed to be, I responded. *"Create what?"* I asked. *"Anything,"* it replied.

I sat there for a long time that day; journaling, and meditating, and conversing with my heart whisper.

Why do I always feel so creative when I travel? Where does this go when I get home? What is it about being in Australia that makes me feel like I've been flipped upside down and shaken, like dumping the contents from the bottom of your purse out to find both the treasures and trash you've been schlepping around for years? Was it Australia or the fact that I had been still and quiet for the first time in years?

A SHIFT IN THE ATMOSPHERE

Late in November of 2019, I returned both refreshed and exhausted from a vacation to Europe that had come on the heels of an extensive period of work travel. I decided that I needed a small break from traveling, so aside from a brief trip to Atlanta to celebrate my 40th birthday with some of my dearest friends, I would stay put in Chicago (where I now call home) for a few months.

By February, my travel schedule again started to fill up: Charlottesville for a week—Austin for three days—a ticket to Orlando to be with a close friend during her upcoming surgery—and the plans continued—until they STOPPED.

"Let's hold off on booking the rest for now and see what unfolds with this travel situation."

I was working in educational travel, and although COVID-19 had not yet impacted US-based programs, it was a very real situation for groups traveling internationally already. We were cutting back on US-based staff travel to counter the costs being accrued by canceled trips and the rerouting of other itineraries.

"We need to cancel your upcoming trips for now, and we can reschedule them when things return to normal." *Normal...* what is that anyway?

Needless to say, those trips were never rebooked, and there I was day after day sitting in my office, surrounded by my art supplies with the backdrop of my travel photos positioned behind every Teams and Zoom call I participated in.

ENTERING THE CHRYSALIS

In January 2017, I had taken a Reiki level one class as a birthday present to myself after a deeply transformational intuitive healing session I received on a trip to Florida. I didn't understand at the time just how transformational it was, but **I heard a much louder voice than a whisper** on that day telling me that it was time for me to embrace and understand my intuitive gifts.

Somewhere **in my gut, I knew exactly what this meant**, but my mind was still in a place of denial and using fear as armor. The words that echoed clearly and consistently from that session were:

"You have to heal the little girl within you."

"You will create something that does not currently exist."

"Find a way to become more comfortable with the gifts you have."

I had signed up for two back-to-back experiences, which consisted of an intuitive session followed by a Reiki session, but what I received was so much more than I expected.

Reiki was the tool that stood out to me at that moment as something I could use as an anchor; something to hold on to while I delved deep into my inner world. It was a beautiful container that helped me throughout this leg of my journey that I had chosen to embark on. What I did not expect to find as I took this leap, though, was that when I really got quiet and still, my creativity would come pouring out of me in ways that I had never dreamed possible.

It really became recognizable when I leaned into my creativity during the first lockdown of the pandemic in March of 2020. It began as a response to boredom. Then the doodles that I've been halfheartedly sketching on my school and meeting notes for decades started appearing in elaborate and intentional ways in my artwork. **My creative voice was getting louder now**, and even as I resisted it internally, external situations began making themselves known, which were harder to ignore and sounded like fun. I started signing up for online art workshops with a friend. I would receive occasional texts from her with a link to register and a note that said, "Come join me!" They were hosted on Zoom, of course, and I had nothing else booked and nowhere to be, so why not? I thought it could be fun to be an art student again after so many years of being in the educator role.

This was the key that unlocked the flood of creative energy that had been building up for decades. The first things that poured out, though, were the usual suspects: frustration, doubt, judgment, disgust—you know them well too, I suspect. Then one night, a miraculous thing happened. I had immersed myself in several consecutive online summit experiences all focused loosely on the concept of creativity. I had spent several days in my office—now office/studio—making art, listening to people speak about creativity, and allowing myself to create in new ways that I would have previously critiqued and resisted.

My sleep schedule had flipped on its head, much the way I felt the year prior in Australia, and I found myself curiously cutting up old journal pages and sketchbooks with an X-acto knife and gluing them onto old unfinished collage works at 2 am. There was no "trained-artist" thought process identifiable here other than something along the lines of "*hmmm, this looks cool.*"

Little did I know at that moment that my artwork was a physical representation of the deep soul work that I was doing in the unseen realms. I was in the metaphorical chrysalis, recreating my whole world through the power of creative energy. I had no idea at that moment that my artwork, my relationship with my soul wisdom, and the part of my identity that I knew as an entrepreneur, were all in the midst of taking a quantum leap that would land each of these aspects of myself firmly together in the present moment.

I was again answering the whisper, and it was returning as an echo that was getting louder and clearer with each conversation. I had heard it calling to me, was regularly engaging with it, and receiving from this process repeatedly more than I could have ever imagined.

Just as I had attended Reiki training and uncovered my creative voice; **when I started to explore my creativity more deeply, I found my soul wisdom.** The practice of creating art started to fill me with joy in ways that I had not experienced in decades. I was creating now, not from a space of resistance or want, but from a need that was bubbling up inside of me that I **could no longer ignore.**

As I sat in my studio at 2 am with my X-acto knife and started cutting up the pieces that I had made earlier that day, something came over me that I can only explain as either a mad stroke of genius or what many who have experienced it would identify as "the zone" or "**being in the flow.**"

The house was quiet, and being amid a lockdown, there was nowhere for me to be and nothing that I was responsible for thinking about other than just existing in the world. Out of the corner of my eye, an old canvas started calling to me.

As I explained earlier, I experience the world through color. Colors become more vibrant or stand out to me, signaling for me to take action in some way. I also hear the vibration or frequency of things. It doesn't happen through words necessarily, but certain items or directions often whisper to me also. **It starts as a shift in the atmosphere;** the sound within a space suddenly gets quieter, or I may hear a soft buzzing, and then I can feel myself being drawn to look for something. As I approach whatever is calling to me, the sound shifts again, or I receive a different kind of clarity (a color pops out, or a word floats into my awareness, etc.).

A perfect example of this is that I generally know when it is snowing, even when the blinds are closed. I will get a sudden urge to look towards the window. I hear the whisper say *"snow"* and a smile appears on my face. When I open the blinds, the snow is falling. On this particular evening, though, it was a canvas that I had worked on years earlier that was calling for my attention.

CREATING HARMONY

One summer during my art teaching career, I decided not to teach camp and set a goal for myself to instead create enough work to have a solo art exhibition. I did. It was held in a local coffee shop in Atlanta (where I called home at the time), and the canvas now calling for my attention was one of the pieces that I had created during that summer. Like is the case with most things, there was a lot of celebration that summer as I manifested my longtime goal into reality, but there was also a lot that was very challenging. I was experiencing a moment along my personal journey in life that was quite dark at times. Knowing this, it is so interesting for me now to reflect on the artwork that I created for that show. I produced a whole series of work based on strong female influencers from my life, all portrayed as empowered, fairy-like creatures with both human figures and butterfly wings.

As I sat in my office/studio at 2 am, I decided to use a technique that we had recently explored in a visual journaling class I had taken online. I started gluing shapes cut from a recent text I'd written on top of my old collages. What resulted was a layered juxtaposition of old and new, living together harmoniously. It brought new life to my old work and deeper meaning into the words I'd recently written, reflecting on my current situation.

Over the next few weeks, I dug through boxes of old journals and sketchbooks, ripping out page after page and discovering parts of myself that I had forgotten had existed in those darker days. I brought them to life again in new ways, through a much clearer lens.

They say that hindsight is 2020. Well, the year 2020 definitely brought me much **clarity** about the journey I'd taken to get there.

I was completely fascinated with all that I was learning through and from my layered collages and decided to experiment with creating something completely new to see what insight I would receive through the process. I had become adept at efficiently achieving a receptive state in my meditation practice and was curious to see if I could achieve it in my creative practice.

I absolutely could. In fact, I see and hear the insights even clearer when I start an artwork while in a receptive state from the very beginning. I had completely transformed my relationship with my creativity; we were now in an ongoing conversation. It was through my creative practices (you could also say: ongoing experiments and play) that **I had learned to interpret the voice of my soul wisdom.** My soul speaks to me in many ways: color, sound, vibration, or energy, sudden and distinct desires to explore a certain place or thing, dream symbolism, and the list goes on. I call these soul languages, and all together, they make up **my unique ways of knowing and being in the world.**

ACHIEVING FLUENCY

I have become fluent in communicating with my soul wisdom through **intentional and regular engagement** with it (my "practices"). I now understand why so many years ago I heard the whisper to go travel. It was on these adventures around the world where I learned to see and hear in a deeper and more receptive way. It is no wonder to me now that I was drawn to teach in schools that embraced the practice of experience-based learning or that I spent nearly a decade creating programs all over the world through my career in educational travel. I was answering the whisper, and I'm so glad I did!

I'm now in a place where I consciously initiate the conversation. As I share my soul wisdom with others utilizing my soul languages, those who communicate in a complimentary way hear the call and engage in conversation with me. Woven into my channeled artwork, intuitive sessions, and soul-guided collaborations are the whispers of soul wisdom that someone else is receiving in their own way, at **just the right moment** along their journey.

ABOUT THE AUTHOR

REGYNA CURTIS

Regyna Curtis is a well-traveled soul wisdom explorer. After spending years in the worlds of art, education, and travel, she transitioned her career from corporate to soulpreneur, creating Atmaitri. Atmaitri is a combination of two Sanskrit words that together can be interpreted as "soul kindness". Atmaitri sits at the intersection of spirituality and creativity, providing a space for those exploring a deeper relationship with their authentic ways of knowing and being. Regyna is a soul wisdom mentor, speaker, intuitive artist, and art channel. She has come to this place through the quest to become fluent in the language of her soul wisdom and now shares her gifts to help others identify and interpret the languages of their own.

Connect with Regyna!
Website: www.atmaitri.com
Etsy: https://www.etsy.com/shop/atmaitri
YouTube: https://www.youtube.com/
channel/UC8MNS1IGyV7Zo_VyFubGUZw
Instagram: https://www.instagram.com/atmaitri/
LinkedIn: https://www.linkedin.com/in/regyna-curtis-1472b47/

RENÉ DEANDA

FOKUS POKUS! MAGDALENE THE DRAGDALENE SAVES THE HUMANS!

Written by René L. DeAnda

Creative Compiler of All Cooperative Components

Creativity can be used in many different ways in the business world; the following story is a demonstration of one of those ways. Through story, the author has introduced Magdalene the Dragdalene, who is the main character of a series of short stories to be released after her debut in this book. The author also takes advantage of the global opportunity to introduce timeless concepts that are now being rediscovered, and ironically are now considered "cutting edge." It is the author's desire that those who read the story will giggle and laugh their way into Magdalene's world and will INNER-stand the basic concepts presented. In joy!

~ ⊚ ~

"*A*ll dragons know how humans work; but most humans don't know how humans work." thought Magdalene the Dragdalene as she pondered how to inform humanity of their best-kept secret. You see, Magdalene is a dragon, and she is my best friend; she wanted to save humanity because I am a human.

All dragons know that humans are actually electromagnetic engines; and that they can attract any situation unto themselves simply by focusing upon it. *Powerful indeed!*

Magdalene set out on a mission to inform the entire world of humans about their superpowers; after all, she knew if everything kept status quo, she might lose her best friend in the whole wide world, and believe me, neither one of us wanted that!

She witnessed how the technology of the time kept people in agitated states of hypnosis and discouraged any kind of independent or curious investigations amongst themselves; the kind of fun and curious investigations we went on every day. We suspected that the entire planet, and all her inhabitants, were subjected to endless abuses by the conglomerates that had, long ago, replaced humans who had beating, feeling hearts; it would be a humongous undertaking to snap every human out of their hypnotic state, but that's what needed to happen to save the humans and Mother Earth. *Magdalene speculated that since the humans couldn't save themselves, it would take a dragon!*

That's why Magdalene the Dragdalene set out to help ALL humans to innerstand how their personal engines worked, explaining to all of them what a wonderful thing it was and how it worked.

She wanted to SCREECH from the highest branch of The Great Tree of Life and use her talents to explain to the humans that they were not just flesh and blood; they were magical machines that could create whatever they wanted. *"But how?"* she wondered aloud, *"How do I tell them in a way that they will INNER-stand?"*

She wanted humans to understand so deeply that they would INNER-stand it all the way to their electromagnetic core.

Up, up, up she flew, her large wings creating HUGE GUSTS of wind, as she flew up to her workshop; her workshop was at the far end of the Grand Hall, within The Great Tree of Life.

The Great Tree of Life was a multi-colored tree that stood in the center of the most beautiful island you have ever seen. The tree reached up to what seemed like hundreds-of-thousands of feet into the sky. Its multicolored bark shimmered in the sun while its golden leaves fluttered in the breeze. The trunk was so massive that it would take at least a hundred humans to join hands around it.

Magdalene flung open her cabinet doors, searching high and low, in boxes large and small, for anything she might use to convey her lesson to the masses. She found trinkets and bobbles and pieces of multi-colored copper wire; she had a fancy for copper wire, so she had tons of it, and because it was multicolored, it would be a great fit! She held it up, and it sparkled in the sun; "yup, it's in!" she snorted aloud and plopped it on her workbench. *She giggled, and little rings of smoke escaped her nose...*

Magdalene was shaking boxes and searching under papers when a few crystal marbles escaped a stuffy old cigar box she used for storing her stamps. She squealed with delight as she tracked the brilliant scarlet-red crystal across the floor... *"The PASSION!"* she exclaimed as the light reflected deep into the scarlet crystal, and it winked at her as it danced its way across the floor. As she held the scarlet-red crystal up to the sun, it flashed with purpose, power, and passion!

The other crystal marble was clear with strands of blue woven throughout; it reminded Magdalene of strands of DNA, and she thought it would be a perfect fit for her little project! After all, she thought to herself, the big secret is locked away in the DNA!

By the time she was finished collecting as many trinkets as she could, she had quite a good-sized pile of sparking wire, crystals, wood, rocks, and the like. Mr. Crow, who never missed a thing (especially when it involved *sparkly* things), happened to be perched just outside of Magdalen's workshop, wondering what she was up to. He invited himself into her workshop and perched himself atop her head; "What *ARE* you doing?" he cackled with utmost curiosity.

"Marc!" exclaimed Magdalene; Marc was his familiar name, but only a select few were allowed to address him as Marc, and Magdalene happened to be amongst the privileged few. "I'm creating a piece of art that will allow me to show the humans how their personal engines work!" exclaimed Magdalene.

*"Why on **Earth** would you want to do that?"* inquired Mr. Crow.

*"Yes, why on Earth **would** you want to do that?"* repeated Sir Pokus as he poked his bearded face through the door. Sir Pokus, the local Wizard, wasn't keen on informing the masses of their gifts, for if they become knowledgeable, they might intrude on his solitude; like any good wizard, Sir Pokus very much appreciated his solitude.

"Well, good morning Sir Pokus', quipped Magdalene as she winked at Mr. Crow, knowing how this conversation was about to go.

"You know," Pokus said, as he pulled on his long pipe, "Hagrid was right." he mustered his best Hagrid voice... *"Why? Blimey, Harry, everyone'd be wantin' magic solutions to their problems. Nah, we're best left alone."* (Philosopher's 51), and then he added in his own voice, "Not only that, but we'd be better off without them! Then we wouldn't have to hide from them!"

Knowing how Sir Pokus despised the unimaginative humans, Magdalene explained how she feared the planet might die at the hands of humans who are simply uninformed; and how it might thrive if someone informed them of their hidden magical powers. She went on to explain how if they didn't do something fast, the humans would soon disappear, and they might disappear too.

"You're wasting your time Maggie; those humans aren't smart enough to grasp the power they hold. Even if you did tell them, they wouldn't believe you, and even if they did believe you, they wouldn't be capable of wielding their own innate powers, at least not in any meaningful way. They'll cause more damage than good!" Sir Pokus shook his head and shuffled off down the hall to find some blank scrolls to scrawl on.

He spent his days honing his manifestation skills by creating the beautiful images he would view through his mind's eye. First, he would draw them on his paper scrolls, then he would think about how it would feel to touch them, to smell them, and to experience them; then FOKUS POKUS! He would resonate so fully with his thoughts and emotions about the images that they had no choice but to manifest into the beautiful reality he had created for himself. *Sir Pokus knew very well how his electromagnetic engine worked; he used his thoughts and emotions to manifest his amazing reality every day.*

"Bwahahahaha" he bellowed as he tried to imagine a human with even a fraction of his imagination, of his power. He shook his head and quickly lost interest in Maggie's pie-in-the-sky project, for he had his own exciting creations waiting to be revealed.

Mr. Crow, on the other hand, listened patiently and finally nodded his head in agreement; "I'll be right back," he said as he flew off into the mid-morning sun, using Magdalene's head as a springboard.

He returned with the most magnificent stone Magdalene had ever seen! It was brilliant red, and it was in the shape of a heart. "Where did you find such a beautiful thing?" wondered Magdalene, *"Did Sir Pokus create this?" she inquired with a bit of hesitation.*

"No, Pokus would never create such a thoughtful stone. It was a gift from my dear friend Mel," said Mr. Crow, "a gift I've cherished for many moons. Tonight, I gift it to you; your special project needs a strong heart."

"Thank you," whispered Magdalene as she humbly accepted the heart of glass.

She knew Ms. Mel very well, and it didn't surprise her at all that the heart originated with her. Ms. Mel also dwelled in The Great Tree of Life, which made sense because squirrels generally dwell in trees, and Ms. Mel was indeed a squirrel. Magdalene vividly recalled the last time she visited her. You see, Ms. Mel is the Town Crier, not in the traditional Town Crier sense, but in the *actual crying* sense.

Ms. Mel had enough tears for everyone living in The Great Tree of Life, happy tears, sad tears, ecstatic tears, bored tears, mad tears, even content tears; she had them all! She had such a HUGE heart and housed SO much emotion that she just couldn't help herself but to wind up in a puddle of her own tears at least three times a day.

It wasn't but a few weeks ago that Magdalene had waited restlessly outside of Ms. Mel's abode. She tapped on the little squirrel-sized door with her oversized dragon tail. Ms. Mel swung open the door and out wafted the most delicious smell of homemade cookies anyone ever did smell! They sat out on a large limb and had tea and freshly baked cookies and laughed, and laughed, and of course, they laughed so hard they cried; after all, one can never leave without first shedding a few tears with Ms. Mel. She thanked Ms. Mel for the scrumptious visit and promptly received one of Ms. Mel's infamous hugs. She pulled Magdalene in with her fluffy tail and squeezed her hard and long! *The best!*

"I'm going to have to go thank her personally," thought Magdalene, as she dreamt of her favorite warm cookies and squeezy hugs.

Marc decided to stay and assist with Magdalene's project; after all, he was handy with machinery and could speed things along... *before Sir Pokus grew bored and began to meddle.*

"Where to begin?" he asked Magdalene. Magdalene found a blank scroll and began sketching out her thoughts. She asked Marc if he thought her blueprints were manageable, and despite his hesitation around some of it, they moved forward.

"Whirrrrrrrrr" went the drill... "BANG! BANG! BANG!" Sounded the hammer.... "I don't know," said Marc as he shook his head. "I thought this was going to be a simple project..." *The blue moon rose high in the sky as they worked well into the night... the whole middle section of The Tree of Life shook with the vibration of the machinery.*

The sculpture came together nicely; a solid, square base with a spiral rising out of the top, electromagnetic tendrils emanating from the spiral, depicting the frequency pulsed out by the beating glass heart tucked inside. The outside was decorated with a bright blue electrical pulse representing electrical thoughts and red and blue swirls representing magnetic emotions. The Great Tree of Life sits on top and is decorated with colorful copper and crystal, orb-like depictions of DNA, PASSION, and a central, magnetic lodestone representing the human electromagnetic engine. Closer observation reveals a peephole in the back; a peek inside exposes the beating glass heart, the heartbeat made of copper, various crystals, metal, wood, water, and air representing all the things that make up the human electromagnetic body.

She found a string of lights that flickered in various colors, and she stuffed them inside her sculpture, "There! That should do it!"

Magdalene bounced up and down with joy when the multi-colored lights inside lit up and scrolled through a variety of colors representing the range of emotions that drive the human electromagnetic engine; the greens were soothing, the blues cool and refreshing, the red inspired, and the yellow was bright and life-giving! The feeling was overwhelming for Magdalene, and Marc was in such awe over her achievement; he ab-SOUL-utley knew it was a product of love.

"Helloooooo! Helloooooo!" hooted Professor Barnes as she flew in and perched on the drill. She was excited and peered over her glasses to see what all the flashing was about.

"Hello, sister! I was expecting you when the moon came up! Come see what we made! And... *How are you?*" she asked, almost forgetting her manners. *"Blessed and highly favored, thank you!"* replied the wise doctor with a wink.

Magdalene was excited to show the professor because the professor had always known Magdalene was born for a BIG purpose, but neither of them knew what that purpose was; until now. The room was bursting with the energy of PURPOSE!

There it stood, in the middle of Magdalene's workshop, the sculpture that would save humanity, light's flashing, heart pulsing, and Magdalene was standing there beaming with pride and anticipation. She gushed out her story about how she was going to save the humans from extinction, and possibly themselves too; Professor Barnes listened intently, nodding her head all the while.

"Wonderful!" exclaimed the professor, *"But what does it do?"* she inquired as she stood admiring the sculpture.

Magdalene took a deep breath and began to explain, in all her excitement, she had forgotten to tell anyone, "It is a demonstration of the electromagnetic body and how it works." She pointed to the sides and exclaimed, "There are pictures of electrical thoughts and magnetic emotions that come together to create the electromagnetic engine that humans are."

She then went around to the back and looked through the peephole, "It has a heart inside that pulses out the frequency that attracts similar situations, people and objects to it. *Just like humans!*" she exclaimed!

"The colors represent the various levels of emotions humans experience, everything from red, representing anger and despair, to green representing love and compassion, to purple representing joy and happiness. I hope that helps." said Magdalene as she watched Professor Barnes' face for signs of innerstanding.

She added, "It is important humans learn this so they can regain control over their society before the conglomerates wipe out all the natural resources, including humans, and quite possibly us!"

"Ah," nodded the professor; her innerstanding was immense. Not only did she innerstand the rationale and the concept, but she also innerstood the importance of teaching *every* human being about the magic they held within, for they *all* have it, and it would take *all* of them to save the planet.

There was a faint scratching at the door... and the smell of freshly baked COOKIES! Ms. Mel had come to see what the big deal was in the middle of the night. She invited herself in, her fancy tail following with a *swish, swish...* she plopped down a huge plate of steamy cookies. Magdalene, Marc, and the professor all explained what was happening, and, of course, Ms. Mel began to cry.

She cried tears of happiness for humanity, as she, too, knew the time had come. She also knew that it would be a time of great revelations for the planet and that much strife would come before the humans really innerstood how to work their magic. She knew some would get it right away, while others would be fearful of it; she even knew there might come a day when the two sides would choose to live apart from one another but would one day come back together in harmony. She knew when THAT day came, she and her friends could share *their* world with the humans, *all of it.*

"Well, if it isn't Sir Pokus!" exclaimed Professor Barnes as she peered over her glasses... He was standing in the open doorway... the smell of warm cookies had wafted all the way to the top of The Tree of Life, where he had been busy imagining and scrawling in his study.

Everyone remained silent as he inspected the sculpture and nodded his head, and stroked his beard. He then rolled out the scroll he had been working on all day and night... Everyone gasped! For he had intricate drawings of *hundreds* of humans, dragons, wizards, crows, owls, and squirrels, all eating cookies and dancing *together* around The Great Tree of Life. It was obvious, Sir Pokus had joined in the quest to save the humans!

"**FOKUS POKUS!**" proclaimed Sir Pokus as he struck his staff to Magdalene's hardwood floor with a **BA-BAM!**. "**It's time!**" He exclaimed as he conceded to save humanity.

The Great Tree of Life shook in agreement as the force of his staff resonated throughout the Grand Hall, all the way down to the smallest root, and up to the tip top leaf.

It was done. The deal was sealed. Everyone was on board, and they commenced laughing, crying, dancing, and eating freshly baked cookies in the center of The Great Tree of Life.

How exciting!

~ ๑ ~

Your attention to this story is treasured and appreciated. Magdalene the Dragdalene resides at InnerstandU.com; there, you can view her sculpture and the illustrations to the story. You will also find her course on regaining control over your personal engine, so you too can use creativity to create your most desired reality!

ABOUT THE AUTHOR

RENÉ DEANDA

René DeAnda, creator of Magdalene the Dragdalene™, energy artist, transformative workshop developer/facilitator, and personal coach. René assists children, and adults, with reclaiming control over their lives. Together we discover what they are currently attracting, what they would most like to be attracting, and how to get there.

The journey begins by innerstanding how our energetic engines work and how to purposefully use our thoughts and emotions to steer/drive them; we then discuss and practice a multitude of tools to keep a highly maintained engine—everything from breathing exercises to reframing a situation. Discovering and applying these skills allows my clients to have a highly maintained engine that will yield a highly synchronous, positive life!

Now is the perfect time to innerstand how **your** energetic body operates.

Magdalene reminds us: if you're not driving your engine, someone else is!

Website: https://www.innerstandu.com/
Facebook: https://www.facebook.com/groups/innerstandu
LinkedIn: linkedin.com/in/rené-deandaɪɪɪɪ
Instagram: https://www.instagram.com/renedeandaɪɪɪɪ/

MICHELLE LEE DESIMONE

WHAT IS CREATIVITY? BEING THE WORST IN THE ROOM AND NOT CARING

*C*reativity is discovering your own magic. . . and owning it. It sounds simple, but for me, it was anything but. I had to grapple through the distractions of the daily grind and decide it was not selfish, it was not a luxury, it wasn't a hobby, it was absolutely oxygen like necessary. My journey took me 35 years to discover what my own magic was. I then had to make a commitment and decision to get in touch with it daily. Plainly put, I was going to suffocate and die a fast and painful death had I not taken the time to find my own magic- like a person desperately fumbling to find their oxygen mask on a plane that is going down FAST. I knew the mask was there. I paid attention during the tutorial before the flight took off. But I didn't think I was actually going to have to use it! Damnit.

For me, a few things needed to happen first: One: I needed to decide I was worthy of finding my magic/ oxygen mask and stop being so concerned about everyone else finding theirs. Yes, I am a recovering codependent—like textbook codependent. Open up a picture of any Psychology book and look up codependent, and my name and picture are there on display. Two: my oxygen mask/ magic greatly benefited my mental and physical health. Three: discovering and touching my magic daily benefits my contribution to the world.

A year ago, I was working heavily with my therapist to do much needed healing when she introduced me to a podcast. This is where I first learned about inner child work. In a deep meditative state six year old me asked thirty five year old me, "why are grown-ups *so* sad?" Adult me answered and said, "adults are sad when they can't find their magic," and that's when this revelation began.

My magic is found in the free-flowing movement of dance.

Some days I get to be so completely immersed in it that nothing else in the world exists or, if it does exist, doesn't matter, including time. Other days I must discipline myself to at least touch it, even if it's just for a few moments before starting my daily hustle. Either way, dancing connects me to the truest and most authentic self and the one who created me.

Please don't misunderstand what I'm saying. I am not a professional dancer, nor do I claim to be. I am not the best dancer in the room, and I haven't even had the most professional training. What I do have is cosmic rhythm flowing through my veins and an immeasurable passion for the beauty of the human body in the free-flowing movement of dance. When I am dancing myself or witnessing this work of art, time no longer exists. I instantly am thrust into another realm that I know I originated from.

I danced as a child, never competitively. I was never chosen for any advanced dance class or travel team. Never won any trophies or awards. Plainly put, I am not even all that good. As an adult, I took a modern dance class at Koresh dance studio in Philadelphia, and we had to do a combo with two other students while the instructor and the rest of the class watched. It was a class open to all levels of experience. The instructor came up to me after the combo was over. My eyes were wide with excitement. After all, I just free flowed beauty and life force through my flesh. I was *sure* she was coming over to offer me a role in the performance company's next show. The instructor paused " Yes?" I said. My eyes wide with anticipation. "How was it? Did I get it right? How'd I do? I nailed it, right?" I gleaned. She looked at me with pity " No, it was all wrong, but I've never seen anyone have so much fun dancing, I didn't have the heart to tell you." then she walked away.

As someone who was easily offended by pretty much everyone and everything, it is absolutely shocking to me that her comment didn't send me into a suicidal depressive episode. It didn't. I almost took it as a compliment. Her words stuck. I heard her but didn't listen. I was having so much fun dancing. I was physically there, in a room where I was in the position to be judged or compared to others. Yet I wasn't there. I was in that space or realm where normal typical Michelle with her ego who cares what people think of her would typically care, and I didn't. I wasn't there. I was somewhere else, in a different dimension, a dimension I've only ever gone where dancing has taken me. And she was right, I was having so much fun... so much fun I didn't care how I looked to her or anyone else because I was in my zone. I had entered a space *touching my magic*. And it was mine, and only mine, a place that uniquely belonged to me, reserved for me with my name it no one could ever take from me. People's approval didn't give it to me, and their approval couldn't take it away. It was there since the beginning of time, created specifically for me to enjoy and explore and be immersed whole heartedly in. That is my place. And I knew that is exactly where I needed to be.

I KNOW WHAT, BUT HOW?

One: I decided I was worthy of finding my magic. More than a year and a half of intense therapy for CPTSD (complex post-traumatic stress disorder) and severe anxiety (that I had conveniently mistaken for being an overachiever) my therapist enlightened me to the realization that self-worth was at the core of all my issues. I did not have what I wanted, needed, or desired in my life because I didn't feel worthy of having it. Once I began to work through my many issues, and I learned I was indeed worthy, I spent months leaning into my passion and discovering that dancing was the air I hadn't been breathing this entire time. What a wild love affair that was, and still is. It was like falling in love for the first time with your soul's mate that has been there since the beginning of time. Dancing was always there. It was always my magic. Deep down, I always knew it. It just took me thirty-five years to own it.

Pre-revelation, in my world, and by my twisted standards, busyness and producing results were rewarded (not twirling around to Shaed). Making space for what set my soul on fire never seemed to make my infamous to-do list. In fact, foreboding joy seemed responsible. I'm ashamed to admit, I prided myself on it. Having fun was for fools, and producing results was for the wise. My days and to-do lists were filled with things that produced vein results like working out to achieve a desired physical appearance, achieving a paycheck, achieving certain success, achieving career status, and acquiring the next material thing. The stakes were always high. Of course they were. I made them that way! My life was in pure adrenaline survival mode, and I was cut-throat competing with everyone all the time, all while losing the war within me moving farther and farther away from my true self. All of the vein accomplishments I achieved never brought me any sense of true fulfillment, ever. Just a good ole checkmark on the vision board and a pat on the back followed by a " what's next ? what now "... with a void deeper than the last. It wasn't until I got still and quiet with myself and my Creator, the one who created me use dance as the door to transcending out of the noise of this world and into another dimension, that I was able to meet my magic and discover it had been there all along.

As I mentioned, I danced as a child. With the costs of classes and recital costumes and the excruciatingly painful fact that I wasn't good enough to stand out and be chosen for the competitive dance team, I stopped before I was a teen. Somewhere in my adolescent years, a perfectionist was born. I then only engaged in activities that I could be the best in. Whatever I did, I had to be the best. In a household where I was rewarded for performing, I adopted the mindset that I am what I achieve. Perfectionism wasn't only a defense mechanism for avoiding pain, shame, and judgment. It was a dangerous and debilitating lifestyle. People pleasing, appearance, success, and status were all ways I sought much-needed approval. I am what I accomplish and how well I accomplish it. Perform. Please. Perfect. In the words of Brene Brown, " Perfectionism is a hustle." I had become a human doing rather than a human being. Which, of course, translated into my adult life and career. Overcoming codependency and perfectionism were two barriers that kept me from my magic for sure.

Two: my magic greatly benefited my mental and physical health. I suffered for years with chronic migraines and back pain. At the ripe age of 18, I moved to LA to become a certified Hatha yoga instructor, after discovering yoga relieved much of my physical ailments. Hot yoga, therapeutic deep tissue massage, prescription pain medication, regular visits to the chiropractor, reiki, acupressure, acupuncture, cupping, herbal remedies, you name it, I did it. It all only provided temporary relief. The physical pain always came back.

We are all made up of energy. I spent my entire life stuffing down and avoiding feeling my feelings for many reasons, and feelings are emotions (energy in motion). That energy got trapped inside my body, and it didn't belong there, causing my physical pain. Once I was brave enough to seek help for my mental health, my physical pain began to diminish. Emotions that I avoided feeling (because I was scared to feel them) got trapped in my body and inevitably prevented me from being able to flow freely and move my body and dance.

Fear had a lot to do with keeping me from my magic. Deep down, I always knew I was meant to dance in some kind of capacity. Because my mind was wired to produce results that resulted in status or income, I brushed it aside as a fantasy. Dancing didn't make sense to me. It wasn't logical. I knew I wasn't good enough to dance professionally or to make a career out of it. Therefore, my mind spit out a big fat "no" stop dreaming whenever I would think about it. The mind is dangerously powerful. Use with caution!

The happiest people I know have hobbies and interests they pursue outside of their careers. They get filled by doing activities just for the joy and pleasure of doing that activity. I was always curious about *those* people. "What was wrong with them?" I would think to myself. The question I should have been asking all along was, "What was *right* with them? What are they doing that I am not?"

I'm still in therapy. I still wrestle with allowing myself to feel certain feelings but am committed to the work. This practice is critical to being able to move my body freely. If my muscles are stiff and I'm in physical pain, I'm going to lay down with a heating pad and stay sedentary, and I'm less likely to meditate, pray, and ultimately dance.

How do I make time for this every day? In the same way I make time to brush my teeth and shower every morning. I incorporate it into my morning routine. It's a part of my daily hygiene. Just like I wouldn't leave the house without brushing my teeth or showering (unless, of course, it were an emergency), I wouldn't leave the house without meditating, praying, and moving my body in the art of dancing for at least a few minutes a day. I need to get in touch with my magic every day. Like any love affair, you want to spend time, give attention to, and get lost in your lover. It's both a want and a need. A necessity and a luxury all wrapped into a perfect little gift with my name on it

FINDING YOUR MAGIC BENEFITS OTHERS

Three: discovering and owning my magic and touching it daily benefits my contribution to the world. My ability to be in touch with my magic allows energy to flow through me freely, allowing me to be creative. It's a moving meditation. Not only does it bring me pure joy and happiness, but it also opens me up to allow creative solutions to life's daily trials and tribulations. We all know they come often and hit hard. Sometimes I find solutions, but most times I find pure acceptance in the fact that there is nothing I can do (or control) in a given situation. I just have to let it be. Let go and let God be God. I find this to be the most powerful benefit of all.

In order for me to silence the noise of the busy world, I need the artistic expression of dance and free flowing energy, allowing original ideas and solutions to come to me. It's not that it comes to me while I'm dancing, it doesn't. When I'm dancing, I'm not thinking about anything. I'm feeling the beat and rhythm of the music and my body as it shifts and flows. It's after I'm finished that my mind and body are aligned. My mind is clear, and I am in a place ready to receive and conquer my day, whatever it may bring.

I also get something out of watching other dancers. It puts me in a trance. It's actually intoxicating.

In my profession, I have direct daily contact with my 17 employees. They have direct daily contact with our 30 residents— tone, inflection, words, and attitude matter. Humbled by my many failures, and I have learned that taking care of myself, being in touch with my magic daily, positioning myself for creative energy to flow through me allows me to show up as the best version of me. It allows me to lead from a place of peace, sensitivity, clearness, and creativity rather than an unrealistic state of perfectionism. I know when the demons of perfectionism are near and roaring their ugly heads when I come across as a stiff dictator needing to speak louder and quicker than everyone else and needing to control and micromanage outcomes. I still struggle with it. It hasn't gone completely away. Now, I'm just aware of it. I can notice it, breathe, pause and make a different choice. The struggle is real, though, and it hasn't gone completely away.

I've noticed a direct correlation between *not* being in touch with my magic and relapsing back into perfectionism. These are the days I've neglected my prayer, mediation, and moving meditation of dance (the things that make me, well, me). And this makes sense because all perfectionism is driven by fear. Fear of not being enough . . . good enough, smart enough, pretty enough, skinny enough, fit enough, liked enough, funny enough, deserving enough, you can fill in the blank. Perfectionism kept me from dancing for more than a decade. I knew I had to dance again, but those perfectionism demons wouldn't shut up— "we'll wait until you're in better shape, until you lose five more pounds, until your business is bigger, until your personal life is more stable." It was burning inside me, a flame that wouldn't go out and always pulled me that I had grown used to ignoring. Growing used to ignoring that pull increased my internal misery. Life was only getting better for me on the outside, but internally I was suffocating. I needed the oxygen only dancing could provide, and once I was bold enough to cross that barrier, I learned I could breathe again.

Google defines creativity as the use of imagination or original ideas, especially in the production of an artistic work. Creativity requires another type of art. The art of letting go. Perhaps this is the most beautiful and freeing of all. Letting go of distractions, inhibitions, fears, limitations, and what others may think. I unconsciously let others define what certain areas of my life should look like, and creative space simply doesn't allow for that. Though letting go is a form of a quiet strength and submission, it's also a fierce form of braveness. It takes great courage and boldness to show the world who you really are and not apologize for it. As someone who has spent the majority of her life apologizing for things that were not her fault, you can imagine the type of transformation that needed to occur for this to take place. I celebrate the fact that dancing is forever ingrained into my DNA, even those times when I'm the worst in the room.

ABOUT THE AUTHOR
MICHELLE LEE DESIMONE

"She could never go back and make some of the details pretty, all she could do was move forward and make the whole beautiful." Terri St. Cloud.

Mother of a miniature malitpoo, Mollie, and Licensed Practical Nurse in both New Jersey and Pennsylvania for 15 years, Michelle is experienced in client centered care. Treating a person's spirit, soul, and body are all concepts at the core of her practice. Having personal experience in loving someone who is addicted, Michelle is passionate about making resources accessible for family members and loved ones of the addicted one. These are the concepts that have inspired her to own and operate five sober living homes in South Jersey.

Email: michelle@gracewayliving.com

GRACE EKALL

THE 'C' WORD: CREATIVITY, NOT CANCER. A LOUD SHOUT OF GRATITUDE

HERE ARE A FEW STATEMENTS THAT HELP ME STAY CREATIVE:

- Emotions either create or destroy confidence.
- My mindset births my reality: that reality either births creativity or not.
- Emotions are a gateway to ultimate health, and our mindset is the key that opens or locks that gate.
- Creativity is a state of mind influenced by the present.

We are all creative beings and often excel at 'foreseeing' our immediate catastrophic future. My 'C' word represents a loud shout of gratitude for:

AWARENESS: Lightbulb moments that change everything! My shout of gratitude happened at the peak of my career.

It's 2005: I am the founder and choreographer of a successful dance company. This privilege allows me to see the world with my child and troop in tow. Then, the worst happens. I'm diagnosed with invasive breast cancer. I feel lost. I'm in tremendous pain, feeling helpless and numb. I live far from home, and I'm a single mum to a nine-year-old daughter. My mother passed two years ago; my father a year after her. At this point, news has spread, and the cards are falling. Few believe I'll make it (their eyes betray them).

My company dissolves. I lose the house I'm supposed to buy because "mortgage" has the word "mort" in it. Rock bottom, right?

Well, there's only one way from there.

Be Creative With Your Next Step.

So, that's what I do.

ACTION - Take the driver's seat to create your next step.

This is where the 'creative juice refuses to flow.' A battle to get things going flares against inhibiting emotions. Fear, anxiety, frustration, anger, sadness, resentment, and guilt. The mind is clouded, the heart is heavy, and hope seems like a waste of time. You appreciate the people who are happy to help, but they can't get what's really going on. Physical pain is visible and well-expressed with words. Emotional pain, however, is felt and likely to be diluted when using words to describe it.

Dancing and moving the body in a compassionate way helps declutter the mind, open the heart wide to possibilities and move you to action. *That's* **Creativity.** Do what needs to be done and talk less about it. Don't say, do!

ADAPTABILITY - Molding the reality of the present with the ability to believe in possibilities. This means believing that what's happening to you and around you is somehow helping you. It means embracing this process.

RESILIENCE - Redefining the scars and asking two very important questions. Is there someone, who knows how to help, who can hold my hand? How can I use my own strength to help others? Every day, life offers us numerous opportunities to create a fresh masterpiece. Yet, we often miss out because we're living either in the past or the future.

HOME - Creativity only happens when you connect with the self: the person within. I'm adept at navigating physical and emotional pain through holistic African dance. If you want to stop feeling restless, helpless, and fearful, say "yes!" to **Creativity.**

ABOUT THE AUTHOR

GRACE EKALL

"Grace Ekall is the owner and founder of the Habits That Heal platform. She's a holistic dance practitioner, health consultant, speaker, radio presenter, and the creator of a healthy hot sauce range. She is teaching busy women how to take back control of their health using dance and helping them to reach their full potential.

Grace brings a unique approach to coaching, speaking, and teaching through her crafted holistic African dance; a health-Improvement methodology that combines mental and physical commodities with everyday tasks.

"Restore your cells naturally to prevent and fight breast cancer and eradicate fears".

BOOK A FREE CONSULT:
https://calendly.com/ekallgrace/freeconsultcall
JOIN our invite only group:
https://www.facebook.com/groups/habitsthatheal/
FOLLOW @habitsthatheal
https://www.instagram.com/habitsthatheal/

LAURA GARCIA

LOST AND FOUND

I used to say, "I am not creative'. What an ignorant and shitting thing to say! We are born creative! The Universe proves it to us every second, minute, day. It is our birth right and innate nature.

Pause and think of every detail that is involved in breathing. This is something we take for granted and we do it without even thinking about it, however **IF** we did it consciously it would change our lives. You can tell what is going on with people just by their breath. It changes according to the emotions/moods or state that they are in. Let's all do it, inhale for a count of 4, pause, exhale for 6, do this a couple of times and you have just reset your nervous system. This simple act that we take for granted , instantly calms you down.

Look around you, out a window, step outside, turn your head, just notice everything: Clouds, trees, flowers and animals. The variety /shapes, sizes and colors is endless. They are everywhere, land, sea, air. Mother Nature is a perfect example to us,creation is all around us.

I was the recipient of a beautiful gift. It was wrapped in a harsh, rough,brutal wrapping but I had the courage and boldness to dig through that to find the diamond buried deep in there.

THE UNWRAPPING

Monday morning, it was a glorious winter day. The sun was bright,warm, delicious, you know the kind of day that makes you want to do something to enjoy it? I took my two friends out for a run , the highlight of their day. We came home happy, stinky, exhausted, my babies had smiles on their faces(dogs do smile), I promise.

I jumped in the shower got in my car and off I went ready to put in 10-12 hours at work, the usual.

I had been driving for about five minutes or so, when I started seeing spots, I rubbed my eyes, not even thinking of the mascara I was smearing all over my face, but that did not help. Eventually it spooked me, I took the first exit and came back home.

I parked in the driveway and just sat there, thinking what the hell was that? Why did I come back? I should have kept going. I decided, since I am home, I will call in sick for today , get some glasses and I will be in tomorrow.

WE MAKE PLANS, THE UNIVERSE LAUGHS

It saddens me to think how unconscious I was.

I asked my son if he would drive me, he said he had to take a shower first. I thought, I am not a baby, I am capable of driving myself.

Hey listen, Before you start judging me, I was in "perfect health". I was just seeing spots, I just needed glasses. I had some time before the appointment, I made my son breakfast and hollered out to let him know I would drive myself.

Down the street I went, when I came to the first stoplight . I could not see what color the light was, this did get my attention. I went back home, **again.**

STROKE OF LUCK

My appointment happened to be with an Opthomologies, which is a medical doctor who can perform medical and surgical interventions (I Didn't know this)

She saved my life! She performed several tests after just a few minutes and asked me how I got there. I told her my son was in the lobby. She walked out and called out for my son. She told him to take me immediately to the hospital as I was very sick. My son looked around her shoulders , at me with questioning and concern in his eyes. I laughed, I actually laughed, I told her I was not sick at all, I just needed glasses, in fact, I said , I just ran 5 miles with my dogs . As if this proved anything. She told me, look, I have been a doctor for many years, I don't know what is wrong with you , I do know it is serious. Your eyeballs are almost completely covered in blood that is why you can not see. She handed me a big beige envelope with the X-rays, and instructed me to give it to them..

I was still not worried, I did go to the ER, just to humor her.

I don't know, but I am guessing that most people would be concerned by now, I was not. I told my son, just drop me off, I will call you when I am ready to be picked up.

DAY ONE , MONDAY

I will not bore you with all the details, the hospital did not know what was wrong with me. MRI, CT, PET scans , blood, urine tests. They poked and pinched everywhere, butt, stomagh, legs, arms, face. I was a living/breathing pin cushion for a long time.

The ER doctor told me he had to do a spinal test. He warned, it is going to take 30-40 minutes, if you don't move it will go faster. I agreed , anything to make it go fast, who wants to lay there with needles on their back, right?

Almost as soon as it started he said, ok we are done. Wait, what? 30 -40 minutes past? Where did I go?

He explained that it takes that long because the fluid comes out one drop at a time, but you, he said, have a gaizer back there. I don't know what you have, I promise you , we are going to find out.

Blood samples went out to three different hospitals. My case was even discussed in the UK!

While we waited for the results, something had to be done ASAP to relieve the pressure from my brain, or I would lose my eyesight, yikes!

There was no time to waste, time was of the essence!

THE SHUNT Wednesday

A small pea sized device that helps reroute cerebrospinal fluid to be reabsorbed was implanted.

ILiterally feel the bump on the right side of my head. I often touch it to remind me what I survived.

RESULTS ARE IN

The day after the shunt was put in, they knew.

I had Factor Five Leiden, deep vein thrombosis. A completely different **INHERITED** disorder in which factor V is mutated in a specific gene, which results in a hypercoagulable state. A blood clot forms in the brain's venous sinuses. And prevents blood from draining out of the brain. As a result, blood cells may break and leak blood into the brain tissues, forming a hemorrhage **hence** , my blood covered eyeballs!

5% of people get clots on their limbs. **I am special** , I got them on my brain! I can not begin to describe what this had us go through.

I think of this as a wildfire! That comes living debris, destruction,and isolation on its path. That is what the first month looked like for us. No silver lining, hope, possibilities of a good outcome come in sight. All we could see was dark, gloom, death. My husband told me two times , they had just gotten home, exhausted, depressed, just wanting to crawl into bed. They were called to get back asap, as they did not think I would make it through the night.

My blood pressure was like a zig zag up and down. They could not control it. All the bells and whistles sounding of the alarms!

I can't imagine, I don't want to imagine ever getting a call like that regarding someone I love.

THE BEAUTY AND MAGIC OF TECHNOLOGY

Had this happened only a few years ago, I would have died or my head would have been cut open.

All they did, inserted a tube, inch its way up my leg, stomach, chest, neck, and head to arrive where the shunt was busy doing its job, giving my beautiful brain space to breathe. Several small holes on my body and an angry red ,thick scar on my chest (which is barely visible now ,(yey! was needed for this life saving procedure.

ROUND ONE SATURDAY

My beautiful boys and husband solemnly walked alongside my bed as it was being pushed to the OR, the energy felt dark, heavy, tense as if they were wearing heavy, wet, heavy, freezing blankets. My sister and her husband with tense forced smiles. I remembered being surprised to see her and told her, you should be at home sleeping, really? Would I be at home sleeping if my sister was having surgery? My boys said their forced goodbye, see you later.

I was relaxed joking with the doctor, he introduced me to his assistants , told them we were in luck as I was A+ health, to which I said not really, if I was I would not be here. He explained that many people have the odds stacked against them and I didn't. Blood pressure, weight, drugs, alcohol, cigarettes , I had none of these issues. This took so long that the "plumber" could not get them all unplugged and they all needed to rest.

ROUND/ SUNDAY

NO MEMORIES

During this one, I had a **stroke** and my heart stopped for just a few seconds. The right size was now paralyzed and had 1% eyesight.

I was like a baby, except babies are adorable . I had to be fed, bathed , wiped , cleaned. One Day a CNA was taking me to the bathroom , I caught a glimpse of my reflection in the mirror, I screamed AHHH! The CNA very coldly said, what don't you remember about what happened to you? No, as a matter of fact I don't . I have no recollection of many things. Visitors, nurses, events.

I was in the ICU for an entire month! with nurses watching me 24/7 and my family living in the waiting area. I had a team of angels, disguised as doctors, nurses, therapists that helped put me back together as best they could.

Another month in rehab to help me learn my new normal outside of the hospital. How to **see** with my other senses , by touch , feel by hearing. I remember very vividly a male nurse. He came to check on me during the night, I was shivering and naked in a corner of the bed . The bed was soaking wet, somehow I managed to take off the gown . Ever so gently as if I were a baby he talked softly to me, assuring me I was alright, he carried me and cradled me all the while softly assuring me I was just find, he put a fresh gown on me, then he sat me on the chair while he changed the bed. I wished I knew his name, so I can thank me for showing me what compassion looks like . It amazes me to think that I was not embarrassed, just felt safe.

Slowly, I started to come back to life. Life returned to a new routine for my family. I would lay in bed and listen for footsteps, I would try to guess who was coming by the sound I heard. I would wait to see them, not because they would feed and take me out for fresh air which they all did. They created a schedule so one of them was always there during the day. I wanted to see their beautiful faces to see if there was life in them.

I had "Our Father " prayer playing on a loop in my brain. I was not saying or thinking it, I don't know where /how but I heard it all day long! I would say out loud SHUT UP SHUT UP! The nurses would look at me and ask who are you talking to? They thought I was losing it

The day before I was to be released a PT came to my house, I came to. She came to see what was needed to accommodate the wheelchair. She made expensive suggestions, my oldest son was following her furiously taking notes so as not to miss any of her suggestions. My husband, very sober, simply nodded. I don't know what was going through his mind. He was now the sole provider, and had 4 people to take care of . He was now responsible for everything

I remember saying all I need and want is a chair for the shower.

I have no idea why I said this. I now know, this was a moment of grace. **I BELIEVE IN MIRACLES BECAUSE OF YOU**

This Is what a doctor told me. She said that when she saw my X-Ray , she said a prayer, she did not think I had a chance of surviving.

RADICAL GRATITUDE

I will be forever grateful this happened to me!

Thanks to this , I was able to discover that for most of my life, I was carrying trauma and I did not know it. This absolutely explains my lack of concern and compassion for myself. I had always assumed that I was like this because I was simply strong and knew how to deal with life. In fact, I was not even living in my body. My body was a talking, breathing empty shell.

I now know what trauma is

I do feel badly for my three beautiful sons and my husband that had to go through this. Thanksgiving and Christmas, when most people are celebrating and enjoying time with family and friends. They were taking stolen naps on chairs.

For me it was a gift. This had to happen for me to BE, DO and have what I am meant to. All the signs were there, I just ignored them. I knew I hated my job. My husband and I were like roommates just crossing paths in the house, I was unhappy and did not know it. I used to drive to work hoping to have an accident and die. I would think, I have good insurance , they will be fine without me.

I Knew nothing about life.

I feel like a baby just discovering all the wonders of life. I look at everything with awe . Inspired and amazed with all of life's amazing creations.

LAURA 2.O

By chance or destiny I discovered self development. I went down that rabbit hole of self discovery. I found out who I am , what I am here to do, what I like /don't like. How to take full responsibility for my life. How to make a decision and stand by it.. How and what I want to spend the rest of my life doing . I found deep profound love and compassion for myself and everyone else.. I am in fact very sensitive all these years, I would say I am not sensitive . My faith woke from it's deep slumber I Had unconsciously commanded. I used to say I wanted to be a nun or a physologiest . I know the Universe is benevolent and has our back **if** only we allow it .

Self development helped me get over the many limiting beliefs and blocks that the patriarch enforces on us. I have gotten over so many but as all human beings, I am a work in progress . This is a lifetime commitment. To be the best version of me that I can be.

This was NOT a traumatic event for me, before it I was numb to feeling or experiencing anything in life. However, I do think it was very traumatic for my boys and husband, as they were fully awake and witnessed everything that was happening to me. As I said, I don't have many memories. I still sometimes ask my husband things regarding this when something pops into my mind.

Life's a journey not a destination.

What is creativity? For me it is being and staying curious, open and available to life. Why is it my favorite word? Such a powerful little word.

No wonder children are always asking why.

I don't ever believe or follow any rule, regulation, limitation unless I ask : Does it serve me?

Is there any good for others?

Will it help me grow?

I did not lose my eyesight

I can not only walk, but recently, I started running!!

I am doing what I always wanted to do. I am a cross between a nun and a psychologist= A transformational Coach! I lovingly hold space for people, listen to people and help them go for their dreams.

My husband and I reconnected, after living like roommates for many years. He did not have to clean me butt but he did, if this is not love, I don't know what is. I reconnected with SOURCE

I discovered that I am very very woo, I love it!

My faith is so strong, I vibrate just thinking about it

Yoga, exercise, meditation, reflection, and journaling are a daily part of my life, non negotiable for me.

My three beautiful sons are doing fabulous

I will ALWAYS put myself first. There is a reason these instructions are given when you are going on a flight. They say, in case of an emergency put your mask on first. If you don't take care of yourself how can you take care of others? You can not give what you don't have. Love yourself first and you will have lots of it to go around, it is like a bottleless cup, only if yours is full first.

I will be forever grateful to my family who nursed me back to health. For the Mayo Clinic who found out what I had

We also found that two of my sons have this gene, but now we are aware and we know it is dormant there. I hope it never awakens in them.

I AM A PHOENIX RISES FROM THE ASHES!

My beloved reading Iam deeply grateful for your time. I wish for you what you wish for you.

The light shines in the darkness, and the darkness did not overcome it! KNOW THYSELF

ABOUT THE AUTHOR

LAURA GARCIA

Laura Garcia is a Spiritual and Transformational Coach. Her mission is to empower , inspire and motivate women from all over the world to bring out their divinity. The master key to this is to acknowledge and remember that we are spiritual beings having a human experience. As humans, we must allow ourselves to experience the buffet of emotion that life has to offer. No permission is needed for this but your own. She is a rebel that dances to her own tune. Living in California, married to her first and only boyfriend, proud mother of three amazing sons. A spiritual junkie, Kabbalah student, yoga and natural lover, and a student for life.

LinkTree: linktr.ee/lauragarcia1414
Facebook: Lauragarcia_24lifecoach
Instagram: @lauragarcialifecoaching
Email: Lauragarcia1414@gmail.com

NICOLE GARRITANO, DNP

CREATIVITY STARTS IN THE HEART

"Unconditional love really exists in each of us. It is part of our deep inner being. It is not so much an active emotion as a state of being. It's not 'I love you' for this or that reason, not 'I love you if you love me.' It's love for no reason, love without an object." -Ram Dass

---

*T*he wind whistled through the open windows of my study. The sun was shining bright on this May afternoon as I sat there on the floor sobbing and comforting my 19 year old Brittany spaniel Kasey and my 17 year old Collie mix Sunny. Today was the day, and I was saying good-bye. I had put this day off for so long, caring for them well past each of their primes. Past what many of my dog-loving family and friends thought was enough. They were my original children. When all of my friends were having kids in our 20s, I rescued Kasey and then Sunny.

The interesting thing is that I never wanted a dog. In fact, as a child, I was petrified of dogs. My Grandma always had a dog, and we visited her almost every Sunday. Every Sunday, you could find me on top of her kitchen table trying to escape the dog while the rest of my cousins played and ran through the house. When I met Kasey, I had no intention of bringing a dog home. My boyfriend at the time and I had gone to the mall to do some Christmas shopping one evening after Thanksgiving. As we walked through the mall, the SPCA had set up an area in an empty storefront. There were all kinds of dogs and cats in there to meet. My boyfriend loved dogs and had grown up with them. He immediately dragged me in, excited to see the dogs.

I stood back and watched him interact and play around with the dogs. Honestly, I wanted to get my shopping done. After about 20 minutes, it seemed like we were finally going to escape when my boyfriend saw a sad dog lying under a table, not interacting with anyone. The dog's coat was reddish-orange and white. His nose was shiny pink, and he had the mopiest eyes I had ever seen on an animal. Not that I had been checking out many animals. The worker told us his story. He had been dropped off very underweight and neglected. He was a bit skittish, so they suspected he had not been treated well. The previous owners had told the SPCA they purchased him as a hunting dog, but he never took to it. The dog slowly slid out from under the table and rubbed up against my boyfriend. Our hearts melted, and the next thing I knew, we were driving home with Kasey.

I had no idea what to do with a dog, and it was a weeknight. I had to work the next day and had no supplies. Instead of Christmas shopping, I was at my boyfriend's parent's house gathering old dog supplies and then buying food at a pet store. Kasey wasn't too sure about me, and I wasn't too sure about him. He had a lot of energy, and at times was scared. He would try to run away. I was not equipped for this. At the time, I was going through massage therapy school. One night I decided I would try to do some massage techniques on Kasey to see if he would relax. He was lying on my bed, and I sat next to him and started massaging his paws and legs. After about 10 minutes, he relaxed on this side, so I worked on his head and back. I ended with his ears, and he was snoring—after that, Kasey was my dog. My companion. My everything.

What I didn't realize at the time was that God perfectly placed Kasey in my life. I now know we have certain animals in our lives that are our soul pets. Our connection with them runs deeper. There is a bond that cannot be explained. This would be my relationship with Kasey and Sunny too. Those dogs would go through so many ups and downs with me that I could never have predicted the night Kasey and I bonded.

I fell so in love with Kasey that I wanted another dog. I wanted him to have a companion to play with while I was at work and run in the yard on sunny days. I grew up with siblings, and it seemed natural that Kasey should have one too. I found Sunny through an online rescue and went to visit her immediately. She was the runt of the litter with tan and white fur and a very uncoordinated puppy. The rescue volunteers showed me her littermates and pointed out of their wonderful characteristics. Sunny's litter name was "Delma." While all of the puppies were adorable, I really felt drawn to Delma. As if Delma knew she was being upsold, she lost her balance, rolled down the hill, and fell in the pond. It was the cutest sight. At that moment, I knew that she was the puppy for me (and Kasey). She came home with me that night, and my brother came up with the name Sunny because of her blondish coat.

Sunny and I bonded in a completely different way. Since she was a puppy, she cried during the night, had to be crate trained, and go to obedience school. Kasey was over a year old when he was rescued and was already housebroken and obedience trained. I had been spoiled. I remember getting up and rocking Sunny to sleep and then gently putting her back in her crate for the night. She was held so much as a puppy that even as an adult dog at over 50 pounds, she still thought she was a lap dog and would make herself at home right on your lap. Sunny was a very sweet and docile dog. She would jump up in the window when she heard my car pull in and would be smiling, showing all of her teeth, whining, and tail wagging so hard.

She and Kasey were inseparable. Truly a pack of their own. Playing tug-o-war, running through the yard, chasing squirrels and bunnies, and occasionally bringing those same squirrels and bunnies to the back door as a surprise. They went through so much with me, from multiple jobs, more education, marriage, death, divorce, remarriage, and parenthood. The constant for me for so many years was my dogs. Always happy to see me and always full of love. They were tied up tight in my heart, and there was never going to be a good time to say good-bye.

I did everything to keep them healthy. I fed them organic food before it was the cool thing to do. They took holistic supplements. I took them on daily walks. I wanted them to live forever. As they aged, I found new supplements. When their appetites decreased, I hand-fed them and made them homemade dog food. When their bladders failed, I put them in doggie diapers. When their legs became weak, I carried them up and down our stairs. There was nothing I wouldn't do for my dogs.

When the time came, it was Sunny who told me. She was whining and yelping one morning, laying next to Kasey on their dog bed. Kasey had not been acting like himself the day before, and on this morning, he was very lethargic. As soon as I saw them there together, I knelt down, and petted them both, and said to Sunny through tears, "Okay. I know. I know what you are telling me. It is time."

There were no words. I had prolonged the inevitable far longer than many pet owners. The next day as they both laid in my lap and traveled over the rainbow bridge, a very large part of my heart went with them. Things changed that day. I had a new sense of urgency to pursue my dreams and goals. One chapter was ending, and a new one was beginning.

The Universe had used these dogs to teach me unconditional love and companionship. They taught me a love for all animals and for elements of nature I had never paid attention to before they came into my life. Kasey and Sunny taught me that when I am determined and serve from love, all things are truly possible. They were and will always be my soul pets, and their timing was divine. Through them, the Universe created a selfless heart within me and showed me that the human-animal bond is a divine creation itself. It is the creative force of love, instinct, and loyalty that is unique to each human-animal relationship. No two are the same.

CREATIVITY CONTINUES THROUGH FAITH

"When I let go of what I am, I become what I might be." —Lao Tzu

It was January 9, 2016, and I was standing in my walk-in closet with a large suitcase opened in front of me. I was packing for a month-long trip of a lifetime over 800 miles from home, but I was scared. How would it go? What would happen? Am I ready for this? My hands were literally shaking as my mind raced with so many questions, and I knelt down on the floor in tears.

Only three days earlier, my husband and I had received the call we had been waiting for—a birth mom had chosen our profile. However, when we received the call, we also found out she was in labor and on her way to the hospital. Our lives completely changed in an instant.

I had been so caught up in the organization of leaving for an entire month and getting dog-sitting lined up that I had not let myself feel all of the emotions. I was so excited and so scared all at the same time. I wanted to jump for joy and go and hide. At that moment in the closet, I let all of my fears and insecurities come flooding out.

As I cried, I thought, "Can I do this?" "Will it work?" "Will she change her mind?" Then I remembered two weeks earlier I had clearly heard in my prayer and meditation time to "prepare the space." My husband and I had a room that we knew would be the nursery, but there were still some boxes from when we had moved in stacked along the walls.

I was on winter break from teaching at the college, so I sorted through my boxes later that day. At dinner that night, I told my husband about my meditation time and what I felt we should do. He is not the type who usually will do what I suggest immediately, but to my surprise, after dinner, he went and sorted through his boxes too.

Two weeks later, here I was, standing in the closet sobbing when I remembered just how quickly things had changed. We were chosen. We were doing this. I had a sense of peace and calm flow through me and a vision of meeting the right people to support us. Then I said out loud, "I can do all things through Christ who gives me strength."

That became my mantra as we set off on our journey across the country. It was the biggest leap of faith I have ever taken. Packing up your life within two days, filling your car with all the baby gear you need, making all the financial arrangements necessary, and driving over 800 miles for a baby you have never seen. It is knowing all the risks involved and saying yes anyway.

Once we arrived, it was a whirlwind of getting checked in at the extended-stay hotel, setting up all of the baby stuff in the room, getting unpacked, and then dressed and ready to go to the hospital to meet our birth mom. I remember before we left the hotel room looking around and making sure everything was just right and thinking, "I am coming back here a mom!"

There are so many emotions involved in an adoption. It was difficult for me to feel joy when I witnessed our birth mom's sadness. The nurse in me wanted to find a way for her to keep the baby and magically make everything right for her. However, as we talked with her, it was clear she had thought this through and had many good reasons to choose adoption. Her maturity and selfless love gave us the greatest gift. There is no amount of gratitude or words to describe the love I will always feel for our birth mom.

I believe our journeys were divinely guided to intertwine at the perfect moment. I know she was grieving when we met and that a part of her will always grieve the loss of being a parent to a child she carried. She made a huge sacrifice by entrusting her daughter to us. I never take that lightly. We made promises to her that day that we have honored and continue to honor.

And when we met Aria and held and kissed her for the first time a few hours later, I had no regrets about taking the leap of faith and trusting in the guidance. It was pure blissful joy.

I am talking, crying, jumping up and down, shouting from the rooftops. She was our soul child and meant to be with us. Her journey to her family wasn't typical, and she is far from typical. But when you truly trust in God's plan, you won't want to be typical.

Holding that baby, caring for her, and bonding with her was the greatest gift, and she continues to be my greatest gift. During our stay at the hotel, I would play lullaby music on my computer, and one song became our song. *A Thousand Years* by Christina Perry was and continues to be my love song for Aria.

"I have died every day waiting for you. Darling, don't be afraid I have loved you for a thousand years. I'll love you for a thousand more." - Christina Perry

https://youtu.be/rtOvBOTyXoo

Leaning in, listening, and following the guidance had brought me to this place, to this hotel, to this child, to this great and divine love story. I learned I could do all things. I can be brave. I only have to listen. The Universe will provide.

Our adoption journey taught me that we all are truly One. Our family and friends surrounded us and sent us off with all we needed to step into parenthood. The staff at the hotel and other hotel guests became our extended family. We lived there a month, and my husband had to fly back and forth on the weekends for work. During the week, I always had someone to talk to, food brought to the room, and open arms to hold Aria. I learned that we are all chosen. Chosen for different paths and different experiences, but still chosen for that which is ours. You will never experience your divine path without stepping all in with faith in spite of the uncertainty.

Yielding to faith and co-creating with the Universe is the most sacred form of creativity. The end result always far exceeds your greatest expectations.

MEDITATION FOR CO-CREATION

Sit back, find a comfortable position, and when you are ready, close your eyes. Begin by taking a deep inhale through your nose and release it through your mouth. Again, take a deep inhale through your nose and release it through your mouth.

On your next inhale, slowly inhale through your nose for a count of 4, hold briefly at the top of the breath, and then exhale through your mouth for a count of 4. Inhale 2, 3, 4. Hold. Release 2, 3, 4. Again inhale 2, 3, 4. Hold. Exhale 2, 3, 4. One more time, inhale 2, 3, 4. Hold. And release 2, 3, 4.

Now, as your breath returns to a relaxing pattern, comfortably settle into the space, you are in. As you settle in, allow your body to relax. Starting at the top of your head, feel your forehead begin to relax. This feeling now moves down through your cheeks, jaw, and neck. Now feel the relaxation move across your shoulders and down your chest and arms, and then into your stomach area. Just breathing and releasing any and all tension. Now the relaxation moves through your pelvis and down each leg into your feet, and finally into your toes. Stay here for a moment feeling completely relaxed.

Now bring your attention to your third eye, the area in the center of your forehead. As you do, imagine there is a projection screen in front of you. On this screen, you see yourself six months into the future. Take a moment and look around. Where are you? What are you wearing? Who are you with? What is happening in your life? How do you feel? Clearly see all of the details. Taking them all in.

Next, feel yourself traveling towards this projection until you have stepped into the scene. Notice what future you have created. How does your future self act when he/she sees you? What advice does future you have for you about your creation? Take time to listen to all of the advice. Spend as much time here as you need.

When you have received all that future you wants to share, give future you a hug, and then begin to feel yourself being gently pulled back through the projection, back into your third eye space. Take a deep, cleansing breath.

And when you are ready, gently rubbing your hands or the sides of your legs. Becoming more aware of the physical space you are sitting in. And when you are ready, open your eyes.

ABOUT THE AUTHOR

NICOLE GARRITANO, DNP

Hi, I am Nicole! I am a recovering academic, personal development fanatic, and lover of all things spiritual.

I have been there searching for purpose in life, burned out and stuck —from people-pleasing to skin cancer to marriage, divorce, remarriage, infertility, adoption, and all the degrees. I have been stuck and unstuck over and over again.

Through my study of human design, subconscious transformation techniques, and healing modalities, I have blended my academic, nursing, and spiritual backgrounds into a unique system, helping others get unstuck and step into their purpose and potential.

My signature Discover, Connect, Ascend system lets me use my magic to help others reveal their magic!

Website: www.nicolegarritano.com
Facebook: https://m.facebook.com/nicole.garritano.902?
ref=bookmarks
Facebook Group: https://m.facebook.com/groups/384767219612994/?
ref=group_browse
Instagram: @nicole.garritano.coach

SUSAN J GROSS

ENTER SUDDENLY... READY SET GO!!!

1 942

Introducing Susan Joy

A new life begins

How do you start? How do you even begin to tell your story? Do you start in the present and go back or do you begin in the past and work your way toward the present? Should I roll the dice to decide, or should I listen to my gut? I'll get back to you soon.

Well, I'm back, and after deep analysis and soul searching, I now realize that my early life experiences have, without question, produced an original and dedicated creative me. It wasn't something I was aware of, it just appeared as life began to play out. It wasn't until later in life that I noticed a pattern. This is how it unfolded...

I was challenged at a young age to decide how I was going to accept and focus on major problems that arose... and here's what I found out. While dealing with a loving mother diagnosed with a brain tumor... A father who gambled and womanized... and a sister who was mean and violent... How was I supposed to process all of this at such a young age? That was easy. I escaped and went to the local movie theatre (1955) with a.$.10 admission. I relaxed and got candy and popcorn to round off the $0.25 I was lucky enough to have. So... I sat back and enjoyed the blessing of the very gorgeous Marlon Brando as Sky Masterson in Guys and Dolls. And because I was really lucky and the theatre was only a few blocks from my house, I got to indulge myself in seeing him at least ten more times.

Sitting in the audience and watching such a handsome cool heartthrob fill the screen was the best experience to soothe my soul and maintain my innocence and calm. I also found peace and spirit while listening to the creative magic of Barbra Streisand's music, acting, and writing ability. I knew I wasn't crazy because as an adult, I heard a Barbra Streisand interview, and she specifically mentioned how she totally melted as she watched Marlon Brando on the screen in Guys and Dolls. Total validation! I also found ways to end up on the happy side of things with my best friend and next-door neighbor Joel. We rode our bikes and skated in the driveway and on the block after school. Joel and I had more quality time when we were given tickets to go to children's concerts at the Academy of Music in town on Saturdays, with Uncle Eugene Ormandy leading the orchestra and explaining everything on stage. How sophisticated! So when I analyze how I developed positivity, it was always my escape into the world of talent and storytelling. Lucky me!! A great alternative to being trapped in reality.

Moving right along to teenage years... life became more worldly... going to dances, listening to Broadway shows, and meeting the love of my life. My real-life Marlon Brando appeared one night at a dance unexpectedly. And because of my professional movie watching experiences, I was able to deal with reality when I was presented with it. I knew it was really happening. There he was, handsome, cool outfit and an air of confidence about him. I still don't understand the motivation and nerve it took, but for some unknown reason (it must have been my sophistication), I walked over to him and asked his name. In the courageous moment, after I spoke with him, I realized he came with a date, and I quickly decided to walk away and avoid further humiliation. I don't remember if I was embarrassed or not, too many details when your heart is beating at an

accelerated pace. Unexpectedly and luckily, a little while later, the real-life Marlon Brando came over to ask me for my landline phone number (of course it was a landline. That's all there was... One phone attached to the wall—it was 1957). I was surprised and excited but didn't know what to expect because he was on a date. As luck would have it, I must have been noteworthy because he called the next night... and the rest is history.

I met him at 15, and we spent the next five years constantly being together... I married at 19 while I was still in college. Alan had just graduated. Two innocent and naive babies. Since we were so young and financially challenged, in addition to school responsibilities, I worked part-time and Alan worked a full-time job training for an executive program. Life was busy, but we each did our part so we could survive and afford food and our modest apartment and, of course, our wire hair terrier who sometimes struggled with us financially and ate Cheerios and water. Bless her! Two years after this rigorous schedule, I graduated at 21 with a degree in teaching. I was glad I was able to handle all the big girl responsibilities of being a wife, student, and employee in a positive way.

Then we were blessed with a major milestone at 25 and 27! I had my wonderful daughter, and suddenly my creative focus shifted. I spent hours and days embroidering and stenciling her name on everything in sight. I focused on making clothes, knitting blankets and sweaters for her, and also as presents to give to friends and family. But the real life-changing creative challenge surfaced at 27 when our son was born. Shortly after delivery, through a series of circumstances, he was faced with life-threatening challenges. And as the months passed, we realized that cognitive challenges would be an issue too. So how do you adjust to a new set of circumstances while trying to create a happy and stress-free life for our daughter? Without even realizing it, we made a decision to live with gratitude and laughter. It was the best choice we could have made. Decisions and problems were viewed and solved in a light-hearted way, and we are now blessed with a 52 years old happy human being achieving success despite major limitations.

When my daughter and son started school at 3 and 5, my 33-year public school teaching career returned to part-time and then grew into full-time positions. Because of constant changes in the city system, I found myself in a number of different grade levels and schools. It was interesting trying to analyze faculties and students and trying to fit into the framework that was there. Once I had my bearings in a school, I realized that sometimes it is hard to be yourself when most people don't see things out of the box as I did. But it didn't keep me from going beyond my class responsibilities, no matter what school I was working at.

In various locations, I started a school newspaper. At another school, I created a yearbook for the 8th graders, and I had each student create their own personal page that truly expressed their individuality and personality. We also raised money to fund trips outside of the area, school dances, and graduation programs. I signed my students up for the Young Playwrights program. This meant a professional actor came to our class and coached all of the students on playwriting techniques. Each student wrote their own original play, and we were entered into a citywide competition. It was the most amazing experience when we went to the presentation of the winners, and one of my students was in that category. There was also the amazing Opera Program which sent a libretto of fabulous operas to the class. Our first experience was Carmen. I brought an assortment of thrift store clothing to class, and we acted out the story in the room. The amazing ending to this was we got to go to the Academy of Music to see the final dress rehearsal of the opera Carmen with the professional actors. It was so wonderful to watch the class experience something totally out of their frame of reference and really understand and enjoy it. I know it really changed their world. I met one of my students as an adult, and he told me after he graduated with a teaching degree, he bought season opera tickets when he received his first paycheck. What could be better than that?

Things were calm, and I thought, moving quietly. Then at 60, a huge crisis was about to unfold. Out of nowhere, I had to dig as far down as I could to maintain my sanity and not become bitter or angry. My husband of 41 years and life partner since I was 15 died. All of a sudden, I wasn't able to smile, and the thought of laughing wasn't an option or even a possibility. I spent a lot of time in bed, and I found it hard to be around people. The noise and movement were very confusing to me, so I avoided public activities at all costs. I also found it hard to stop mentioning to people unsolicited that "My husband died. "This unusual behavior of mine taught me you definitely have to bottom out and go with the flow before you reach any semblance of reality or normalcy. I really didn't have anyone I knew who was experiencing such a loss, so I was left to my own devices. I knew after a while that I couldn't continue to live this way, and eventually, I realized that in order to start to heal and return to some semblance of normalcy, I would have to learn to smile again.

So, I turned to what I knew—funny. I started to watch Wanda Sykes, Billy Crystal, Ellen DeGeneres, and other comedy movies and specials. Eventually, a smile and a giggle began to appear. And for life inspiration, Joyce Meyers and TD Jakes's sermons filled my head with necessary positivity and guidance. As I slowly absorbed my new exposure to lightheartedness, my reality started to lighten. It also made me realize that Alan would be proud of me for gaining strength and enjoying his memory.

As the weight lifted, I was freed up to start healing and to slowly rejoin the planet. I found the inspiration to stop wallowing, and I was able to begin writing in my favorite poetic Dr. Seuss style. All through my life, whenever there was an occasion, I would write one of my original poems in simple Dr. Seuss style to help with the celebration. It always went over well, and I always got the feelings and emotions expressed in a simple and easy way. As I continued to journal and get my emotions together, I had a great idea. At that point, I started to look through books on widowhood to see if I could find some emotional relief and guidance. I wanted a book of rules so I could feel better. Oh no... Three hundred pages? Even one hundred pages was too much to deal with, so my creativity broke through!

I knew widowhood was never viewed through Dr. Seuss' eyes, and I also knew through my experience that when you are in deep grief, you are not in the mood for reading a book that lectures or gives you a recipe on how to live. I thought in order to feel lighter, it made sense to me to walk people through reality without throwing out opinions or judgment. I decided to create a safe, non-judgmental space of real understanding. As I was working on writing and strengthening myself, I realized that maybe I could share my ideas and insights to help others heal and feel lighter. As I devoted time for healing, the simple words and thoughts poured out of me. I was able to organize my experiences so that I could document and relive what I had experienced in an easy way. I realized that because of its simplicity, it would be perfect if the

book could be illustrated in such a way that it would feel non-threatening, relaxing, and beautiful all at the same time. I approached a friend of mine who is an amazing artist. She is the kind of creative person who can dig deep and find a way to express ideas in a beautiful and simple way. I approached Marlene Adler, and luckily she loved the project and brought my words to life. The pages are beautifully illustrated with insight and love. Each emotion is given importance, and reality is rewarded and accepted.

I am very proud of the way "Someone Used to Love Me" turned out, and I realized that the story doesn't end after the first year of grief, so I continued to track my progress. I saw my life was leading to a place of more strength and life rebuilding. With Marlene's help and my insights... I Think I Turned the Corner... hit the shelves to give encouragement and hope to people who are dealing with the loss of a spouse. Losing a spouse is not like any other loss because it puts you in a position where your whole frame of reference is out of balance. When you experience other losses, you still have your same life structure, but a spouse changes the playing field. It made me feel good to create books that are simple, beautifully illustrated, and require very little concentration. I am happy that I am able to show that it is possible to work through trauma and reality to find peace. I never thought I would be able to heal, and I never thought I would be able to pass it on in a positive way. I AM VERY GRATEFUL!

Presently my greatest creative venture is working with a wonderful group of women who are regulars in my widow's group. When I think back as to how broken I was after Alan died, I could never imagine myself having the strength or the will to want to take on such a responsibility. It sort of evolved out of my search to find answers for myself so I could function in some way and get out of my bed and return to the world. I joined a widow and widowers group and found myself bored and totally unmotivated when all the members ever spoke about was their grief and inability to go on. I was tired of hearing about it. I thought maybe I wasn't thinking clearly and that this whining and complaining was just the start of a healing process, so I stuck it out for a while. But it never got any better, and I thought... I could be miserable by myself—I didn't have to drive 45 minutes one way to meet with people who enjoyed being victims.

I thought real hard about how to improve this situation, and I came up with a plan. I was able to get a group organized at my synagogue with a professional leading the group. Since we had more control of what the group discussed, we did begin to make some progress. But when the group ended we still felt the need to continue because we needed more on an ongoing basis. We realized as time goes on, life presents different challenges, and we felt we needed each other for support and guidance. I went to the membership person at the synagogue and asked if our small dedicated group could continue. She totally surprised me by saying, " sure, if you lead the group!" Did I hear right? If I lead the group! How was that statement possible? I was still widowing... I thought it over, and since I wanted the group to survive, I said okay. That meant I had to get myself together and plan some interesting stuff.

I pulled out my creative ideas that were meant to take the women out of their own heads. I wanted to make them and myself remember who we were before we were even married. Who we were and who we could still be after all our experiences. I put on my teaching hat and pulled out boxes of memories, and I worked in a different way to help us find our path back to celebrate our originality and find ourselves after such a huge loss. People don't realize when you lose a spouse, you lose your entire frame of reference. It sounds like a simple statement, but that is a huge mountain to climb.

We went out of the box and wrote haiku poetry, we created art, we did chair yoga, and we had adventures. We learned to meditate and live in the moment and celebrate and like who we are. It is a challenge but so rewarding to see the growth and strength that rises up! It is a blessing! I am always amazed that they actually listen to me and follow my sometimes weird requests. They work in groups and do play-acting, and they get involved with some really interesting speakers. We have become really good at expressing ourselves with original writings.

I'm thrilled and definitely surprised when they keep coming back. A Lot of my ladies are so connected that they come for years, and many travel together and hang out with each other on a regular basis. We're a happy non victim talented community of INTERESTING WOMEN who just happen to be WIDOWS!

What a coincidence! Luckily we found each other.

THANKS MARLON FOR GETTING THE SHOW STARTED!!!! MUCH APPRECIATED! AMEN! AMEN! A million times!

So if I have to analyze what CREATIVE means to me it would be

C colorful community

R real ready
E eager energetic
A alive adventurous
T talented thankful
I inquisitive itchy interesting
V victorious variety
E enthusiastic encouraging exciting

ABOUT THE AUTHOR

SUSAN J GROSS

Susan J Gross has spent her entire life learning to implement positivity and strength. She is a retired Philadelphia career teacher who spent over 33 years motivating and exposing students to the world outside of the box. She always focused on how creativity and openness can be life-changing. Her main goal was always to raise self-esteem and self-acceptance in every student.

When her lifelong boyfriend and husband passed away in 2003, she could not continue as she was, and she had to retire. After working very hard to regain balance, she got her spark back. Susan decided to use her experiences to motivate and enhance the lives of other widows. She is putting her passions to work, helping other widows find strength, passion, and laughter.

Susan has two wonderful children, a great son-in-law, and two fabulous grandchildren.

Books:
https://www.amazon.com/Someone-Used-Love-Me-positive/
https://www.amazon.com/Think-Turned-Corner-Someone-Used/

NICOLETTE HALLADAY

CREATIVITY IS HOPE TRANSCENDED

To me, creativity is the ability to see a new path, a new life, and new opportunities. It's the brink of a new adventure with unlimited possibilities on the horizon—this place of potential that I have visited so often throughout my existence. When life feels dull or just not quite right, I sink into this creative energy to imagine and explore what other realities I might be missing. This creates a spark that simmers in me a new excitement and makes me feel alive again.

That's one of the reasons I've been drawn to the path of entrepreneurship. Entrepreneurship insists on creativity for its lifeline. If you aren't creating, exploring, and dreaming, the heart of the business will stop beating. My entrepreneurial journey has been long and twisted, with lots of starts and stops, side gigs, and full-out business operations. But my favorite place is always at the beginning, where the idea of the project is born because that is the place where anything can happen. Bringing that vision into reality is where hope is transcended and is what literally creates the world we live in.

But this new lifeforce birthed from creativity isn't reserved for the entrepreneurs among us. No, it's for anyone who's imagining something new. Whether you're applying for a new job, switching careers, searching for your next home, preparing for the arrival of a new baby, visiting a new place, starting a new hobby, entering a relationship, or even buying an outfit that makes you feel brand new. It's the anticipation of what could be that stirs up that magical creative energy, waking us up to the fact that what we envision can become true.

Going through life on autopilot and not taking the time to think about the kind of existence we actually want to be experiencing can stick us in a rut. When you're stuck on that hamster wheel, buried under responsibilities and just checking things off the never-ending to-do list, life can feel mundane and hopeless. It's in this place where creativity goes to die. And trust me when I say this—I know how easy it is to find yourself there. The good news is, breaking out of that state of being is as easy as rekindling your imagination and allowing yourself to consider, explore and then pursue the start of something new.

Creativity is the ability to dream about something and the courage to take the leap into the unknown even when it feels scary. In that anticipation, creative energy will percolate, and that force can transform your reality into anything you want it to be. Then it's just up to you to show up for it fully and birth that creation into existence. And that is why to me—creativity is Hope transcended.

ABOUT THE AUTHOR

NICOLETTE HALLADAY

Nicolette Halladay is the founder of Inspired Hearts Publishing—an independently owned publishing house focused on multi-author book collaborations, created to share the unconventional and heartfelt stories of entrepreneurs. Giving business owners a platform to tell their stories, own their talents, and leverage their personal story to grow their business.

She started her entrepreneurial journey by launching a virtual assistant agency where she learned the fundamentals of online business and found her love for publishing through niching down in her business and exclusively supporting other female-owned publishers in the backend of their business until she took the leap to branch out starting her own publishing company.

Nicolette does the work she does because of the time, financial and creative freedoms offered in entrepreneurship and her love for this work that pushes her to explore and express total and complete self-expression of the heart and soul for herself and her clients.

Website: www.inspiredheartspublishing.com
Facebook: https://www.facebook.com/nikki.richardsonhalladay/
Instagram: @lovenikkihalladay

DIANE HAZELWOOD

SIMPLICITY OF EXPLORING YOUR PASSIONS

When I was asked to be part of a multi-author book about creativity, a world of ideas came flooding into my mind. How was I ever going to be able to pick just one of these concepts? But after weeks of serious contemplation, I realized all my ideas had one common factor. They were all driven by passion.

Creativity, to me, is the outward expression of one's inner passions. The way we express this creativity is unique to each individual because we are all so very different. Some like to read. Some like to write. Some like to paint. Some like to sculpt. Some like to sing. Some like to dance. Some like to garden. Some like to cook. And some like to travel and explore the beauty of the world and all it has to offer. It all comes down to what your inner dialogue is trying to tell you. Every thought your brain conjures up contains a potential passion. A potential opportunity to creatively express those passions. And a chance to incorporate them into your daily life. The creative voice is most likely talking to you at this very moment. Are you listening?

You may be thinking to yourself, how does one figure out what they're passionate about? Well, I have found that learning what your passions are, and finding the desire to explore them, is actually a unique yet fairly simple equation:

Think it.

- A thought pops into your head. That's passion!
- Feel it?
- Does this thought move you in any way? That's desire!
- Live it!
- What creative outlet will allow you to express this desire?

In November of 2014, I bought a small hair salon from a woman I used to work for. Anyone that knows me would most likely agree that making this purchase was the most "stable" thing I have ever done in my life so far. I've always been a bit of a rolling stone. Which I will later come to realize is not necessarily a negative trait.

Most people would assume that the majority of my creativity lies in me being a hairstylist; when in fact, being so is just a small outlet of my creative world. Fortunately, and unbeknownst to me at the time, this single spur of the moment decision had started a fly wheel of events that allowed me to roll right into my most creative outlet. Exploring. Exploring people. Exploring places. Exploring concepts. Exploring hobbies. Exploring physical activity. But most importantly, exploring my inner passions.

Here are three of my life stories, all having happened over the past few years, that put into practice the conceptual equation of exploring your passions and what that can do for your overall well-being.

STORY 1:

In late 2017, I was cutting my cousin Mark's hair, and he was telling me about a trip he had just come back from. He had attempted a three-day climb to summit Mt. Rainier in WA. He was disappointed he was unable to summit on that trip but was eager to return. His interest to try again was admirable, and I found myself thinking, "it must have been a pretty awesome experience if he is willing to do all that is necessary to prepare for such an excursion over again."

For whatever reason, probably fate, I was moved and inspired by his determination to get back in the saddle. So I invited myself along on his journey.

Fun fact about Mt. Rainier, she is a "sleeping" volcano that stands 14,411' high. Having been raised in NJ, I could not comprehend how tall that was. How could I? I had nothing to relate her to. Needless to say, I had NO idea what I had just signed myself up for. Until one weekend, I went skiing with my parents in Killington, VT. My family and I had been there a bunch of times while I was growing up (come to think of it, my dad never took us anywhere else to ski), and since that was the only real mountain I had ever experienced, I just assumed it had to be close in elevation to Rainier. I was wrong.

"Mom, why do we always go to Killington to ski? Doesn't Blake ever want to try somewhere new?"

"No, he likes that it is the tallest ski resort in VT."

"Oh, cool. How tall is it."

"4,236'."

Well, you can see where that was going.

I spent seven months training for this mountaineering expedition. By the end of June, I was able to climb 1,000 vertical feet per hour, five hours a day, for two consecutive days. I was able to do so while carrying a 40lb backpack. And I was also able to while wearing an oxygen deprivation mask. This mask allowed my body to become acclimated to performing strenuous activity while having a lack of oxygen based on the altitude I would be climbing in. Needless to say, I was in the best shape of my life.

All that being said, I did not summit Mt. Rainier. The night before the big push to reach the top, our guides gave us a quick pow-wow on how the next 16 hours were going to look. "I'm not going to tell you the exact time we will be waking you up because that all depends on the weather. But expect it to be around 3:30am and expect it to be sub-freezing temperatures with 40+ MPH winds. When we are up there, we are going to stop every hour for water and a 300 calorie food break. When we do, I want to immediately see you put on your puffy (for those of you that don't speak mountain slang, your puffy is the biggest and warmest yet most compactable jacket you will ever purchase) with your water and snack in hand within two minutes. If I see you so much as fiddle with your zipper, we will turn around."

At that moment, I made the decision to stay put at this particular junction for three reasons.

1. Even though I was physically capable of continuing, what if, for whatever reason, I was unable to summit. Mark and I were tethered together to a guide at this stage of the climb, and if our guide decided to turn us around because of me not having my snack in hand fast enough, I would be the reason Mark would miss out on his second attempt at the summit. That was not okay with me.

2. For the sake of being too descriptive, blue bag. If you don't know what that is, look it up. For anyone that is a regular 8am kind of person, you will understand immediately.

3. My passion was never to summit. It was to explore and experience.

To this day, I do not regret my decision to stay at camp. Being able to drink my morning coffee at sunrise above the clouds in complete solitude was an experience I wouldn't trade for the world.

Moral of this story:

Think it. Could I climb a glacial mountain?

Feel it? Well, if Mark can do it, I can do it.

Live it! I may not have gotten to the tippy top, but this experience was one of my favorite moments in life. And I now have a list of the highest peaks in each state that I am slowly ticking off one by one.

STORY 2:

A few months after my return from Washington, my friend Jordi called me on a rainy Saturday afternoon and asked me if I have ever been rock climbing. Thinking this might be something I would enjoy now that the fire for trying new things had been lit, I agreed to meet her. Because it was both our first time, we were accompanied by one of the employees who started us off on what they call the "party wall." Now in case you are unfamiliar with rock climbing, the "party wall" is the wall they use when a 10yr old decides to have their birthday party at the rock gym. The handholds are all funny shapes and faces. I believe there is even a panda bear hold. The wall itself is half the height of all the other routes in the gym. And to be honest, it is and is meant to be incredibly easy. Or so I thought.

Jordi went first. She did a great job! I don't believe she made it to the top, but she got pretty close. She was lowered down once she reached her limit, and everything went on without a hitch. My turn did not go as smoothly.

I was only 10 feet off the ground when a panic attack set in. I was convinced this employee was unable to hold my body weight even though I watched him perform the same task with my friend. There was no amount of reasoning that was going to get me to let go of this wall. However, after three minutes of laugh-crying (I'm sure we have all experienced that emotion before-and if not, consider yourself lucky. It's not a good look), I had no choice but to let go of the wall. After an extended period of time practically hyperventilating, your body loses its ability to hold on any longer. To my surprise, but to the employee's knowledge, he lowered me slowly and safely to the mat. Once I touched my toes to the mat, I melted into it like a rubber band. My body had released such a surge of adrenaline that I physically could not use my limbs. Jordi even had to open my water bottle because the use of my hands was nonexistent. I looked up at the rock guide and said, "This must happen all the time here, huh?" His reply, "I have never seen that happen to anybody. And we do kids parties here".

Once I regained feeling in my face and legs, I marched right up to the front desk and signed up for a one-year membership. I was NOT going to let that be my one and only rock climbing experience. I was not going to let an irrational fear stop me from doing something exhilarating.

Moral of this story:

Think it. Let's do something different, like rock climbing.

Feel it? Oh, I felt it alright.

Live it! Since this experience, I have not only hired guides to climb the Gunks in New York and Seneca Rocks in West Virginia; but I have also started dabbling in ice climbing the White Mountains of New Hampshire. I typically spend two weekends a month either traveling to climb sites or taking courses on how to climb on my own. I am currently training for an expedition involving glacial navigation of Mt. Baker in Washington. The embarrassing moment I shared with Jordi that day at the Gravity Vault has opened so many doors. And the desire to explore more options just keeps flooding in.

STORY 3:

Shortly after rock climbing became my new hobby, I had been invited by my friend Serena to white water raft a Class V rapid in West Virginia. For those of you that don't know, Class V is the most difficult to navigate and, in turn, is the most dangerous. Adventure seekers from all across the world come to this particular spot every September/October to raft what is known as the Upper Gaulley. What makes this particular spot so appealing? Every fall, water is released from the Summersville Lake Dam, and floods the Upper Gaulley, creating six weeks of high intensity Class V rapids. Once the dam's water has finished draining into the river, the river only hosts up to a Class III. Needless to say, this particular spot in West Virginia is a hub for all rafting enthusiasts.

My four boat mates and I made it through three of the five Class V rapids on our route before tipping over at the beginning of the fourth (which just so happened to be the longest rapid of the day). IT WAS TERRIFYING. I have never been so scared in my entire life. I have never been in a wetsuit before, so the weight of that pulling me down in the water was new for me. I also have never been IN the water with a life vest on. Sure I've worn them before for safety purposes but was never unfortunate enough to have experienced using one. Between the weight of the wetsuit pulling me down and the buoyancy of the life vest pulling me up, it not only felt claustrophobic, it felt like I was being pulled in two different directions. But one direction was certain, I was heading down river while body surfing an extremely dangerous rapid. I was tossed like a rag doll for what felt like hours. In reality, it was only eight minutes. The adrenaline that surged through my body made it almost impossible to take a deep breath. Which I was desperately trying to do in between being sucked under. An event that happened at least three times. The sound of the rushing water was deafening. But surprisingly enough, the temperature of the water (around 50 degrees F) was the least of my worries. One of the times I was pulled under, I got stuck under the other group's raft. I knew I was at the surface, but this surface was larger than my wingspan and made of rubber. I banged on the underbelly of the raft a few times without prevailing, and I thought to myself that for sure this was the moment I was going to drown. I remember thinking, "my mom is going to be PISSED." In the end, I made it to an eddy —the calm breaks in the river before the next rapid. The feeling of complete helplessness was overwhelming. But the feeling of surviving was incredible.

Of course, I shared this story with all my friends, family (except my mom. Sorry mom), and clients, and they all asked me the same question. Why didn't I just get my feet wet first with a less challenging rapid before attempting the hardest type of rating? My answer to all of them was the same. Nothing will prepare you for rafting a Class V except rafting a Class V.

Moral of this story:

Think it. White water rafting sounds like fun.

Feel it? Class V does sound scary—but I am intrigued.

Live it! Although I will NEVER raft a Class V rapid again, I am thankful for the opportunity to cross that off the list of life. But more importantly, I am thankful I lived to tell the tale!

For most of my life, I assumed I had anxiety and depression. I have always had racing thoughts. I have always felt the push and pull of my inner dialogue. I was always over-analyzing every idea that popped into my head. And it was exhausting. I came to realize I was anxious because I was full of ideas and passions, but was not acknowledging them and letting them out. Once I experienced what it was like to live out an idea like Mt. Rainier, the voices got louder. After living out the idea to rock and ice climb, the voices got even louder. And after surviving the Upper Gauley, the voices got louder still. But instead of being overwhelmed by anxiety caused by all the voices, I have come to embrace each and every one as a new avenue by which to explore a passionate life which now seems to have no bounds.

Now not every anxious thought I have is a passion trying to present itself. Sometimes it's an annoyed family member calling to complain about another family member and they are expecting me to find them a solution. Or it's an issue with a disgruntled client or coworker. Sometimes it's as simple as getting a parking ticket or having a computer malfunction. The list can go on and on. But instead of letting these day in and day out circumstances overwhelm me, and instead of over analyzing them, or instead of taking medications to silence them, I just listen to them. Accept them for what they are. Then let them go. None of these mundane things have the same power over me that they once had.

It's not that rock climbing and mountaineering have "fixed" me per say, but there is definitely something to be said about being in a life-threatening situation (but also in a controlled environment or calculated risk one might say) that has allowed me to see that the everyday nuances are not something to be bothered with. It's just worth my energy. Now, I know that being in life threatening situations is not everyone's cup of tea. But they are my tea. And I plan to drink as much of that tea as possible! That tea has given me the power to fix my anxiety and depression just by allowing myself to become the person that I was always meant to be.

These adventures have changed my life. No doubt. Every door that has been opened since my initial decision to climb Mt. Rainier has presented another bigger and better door. I feel the world is truly my oyster. The amount of love and gratitude I have every day, all by just listening to myself, is remarkable. Think about what you can accomplish if you took the time to pay attention to the little voice inside your head.

I began with this; it was with us along our storytelling journey and so I will leave you with it as well.

Think it.

Our brains are constantly going a mile a minute. Do yourself a favor. Every once in a while, stop and take a moment to truly listen to what it has to say.

Feel it?

Does what your brain conjures move you at all? If you're not listening to your emotions, you'll miss it's attempt to build the desire to fuel the passion.

Live it!

Passion and love are fueled by the same fire. Creativity. And that creative fire is what makes our lives worth living. The only thing that is stopping you from living and loving the life you desire and deserve...is you.

ABOUT THE AUTHOR

DIANE HAZELWOOD

Diane Hazelwood was born in Charlotte, North Carolina in 1985.

After moving to New Jersey, she spent her childhood dancing ballet at a local studio.

In high school she performed in numerous musicals and led the Silvertones, Sterling High School's traveling show choir. It was here that her love of travel was established.

She attended Rizzieri Aveda School for Beauty and Wellness in 2003 and in 2008, she joined Norwegian Cruise Lines to travel the Mediterranean while providing hairstyles for both passengers and crew.

In 2014, she took over Personal Expressions Hair Studio in Haddonfield New Jersey where she continues to specialize in curly hair and organic coloring and products.

After summiting Mt. Rainier in 2018, her passion for extreme sports was born. Since then she has added rock climbing, ice climbing and mountaineering to her life resume and as one door opens to the next, it seems the sky's the limit.

Website: http://personalexpressionshair.com/
Email: dianehazel85@gmail.com

PAUL HEMSTREET

ADJUSTING THE LENS: A PRODUCER GETS
HIS OWN CREATIVITY INTO FOCUS

I squinted as I emerged from the cool, dark editing bay into the hot, blinding sunlight in the parking lot outside. It was my first day on the job, and the other editors convinced me to take a break—they all wanted to see the solar eclipse, which was just starting to dim the edge of the sun. A small crowd of production staff, editors, and crew gathered around a makeshift viewing device rigged up by the prop department using foam core and duct tape. When I finally had my chance to look through the viewer, a furry arm tapped on my shoulder. I turned to see a smiling prehistoric "cave boy," furry from head to toe, accompanied by a teen girl wearing a buckskin tunic, her long hair pulled back tight and wrapped around a bone. The "Pakuni" boy was named Cha-Ka, and the girl, Holly Marshall. She had gotten lost recently on a routine expedition with her brother Will and father, Rick. Unusual, yes, but this was the production headquarters of "The Land of the Lost" TV series reboot, somewhere between Hollywood and our prehistoric world. I knew then this was no ordinary business, and I loved it. The career I had embarked upon would never be ordinary, from my first job to the present.

I sometimes wonder what led me to seek out a creative life in the world of entertainment. Nobody else in my family had. I enjoyed many different activities and subjects in school and often turned to films and performing arts like acting and playing the piano because the experience affected both my heart and head. Some friends had clear ideas of what they wanted to do in life at an early age, while I couldn't make up my mind because I liked so many different things. It wasn't until many years later that it became clear to me that working in entertainment would be perfect for me because there is such a huge range of creative jobs necessary to make the constant flow of films, shows, and performances to feed the public's insatiable appetite. The varied possibilities were endless.

I made a leap of faith during my senior year at Carleton College in the bucolic town of Northfield, Minnesota. I was on a pre-law path with a Political Science major. My work-study job was in the theatre, rotating through the costume department, scene shop, and box office. I was also an actor in my spare time and was president of the student theater organization. That Spring, I was cast in a major role in the musical *The Pajama Game*. At the same time, I was applying to a post-graduate program to be a page in the German parliament or Bundestag. I had previously spent the Fall of my junior year in Germany and was fluent, so it seemed like a great opportunity. They were holding interviews in Chicago that Spring, and it turned out to be the very same day as the final dress rehearsal for *The Pajama Game*. I knew there was no way I could miss that – I couldn't let the cast down. I didn't go. I realized my heart was more into the show because it brought me joy. Until that point, I hadn't taken theatre seriously as something to do for a career. It was the first time I changed my life path to do what I *loved* rather than what I felt I *needed* or was expected to do.

After that, I abandoned the idea of going to Law School and instead found a job in Minneapolis working for a small theatre company as box office manager. I was nervous about telling my parents. I laid out my plan and reasons over dinner on their next visit, apprehensive of what their response would be. They couldn't have been more supportive. That was a major turning point in my life, and it led to me enrolling in grad school at CalArts and moving to LA. I packed up as much as I could into "Suzanne," my '76 green Chevy Vega, and headed across the county to a new life.

I don't believe creativity is exclusive to the arts. Every person on this planet can tap into creativity to live their lives to the fullest, doing whatever they do. Simply put, **Creativity is *thought* moving into action.** It is the birth of an idea that takes physical form. It takes creativity to solve most problems because our world is filled with infinite variables and situations. Most things in the real world aren't exactly the way they are in a manual, and it takes creativity to find a new way of doing things or to make something with limited resources, like using ingenuity to repair your torn backpack with a shoelace when you are on a hike, miles from any store. Creativity is used to figure out how to get your vegetable garden to grow despite the lack of rain, scorching heat, and numerous pests. Or what to make for dinner when your refrigerator is nearly empty. Or finding a way to talk to your children to get them to understand a complex problem. Creativity comes in unlimited forms, yet many people don't feel comfortable being called *creative*. In their minds, creativity lives on a pedestal, only attainable by "real artists," famous musicians, chefs, movie stars, designers, or writers, and so on. I've had so many people tell me, "I don't have a creative bone in my body." I don't believe that. Everybody has creative abilities, but like learning a language, playing a sport, or getting in shape, it takes practice and self-discipline.

CalArts was a hotbed of creativity. I was in the Directing program for Theatre and Film, led by Alexander (Sandy) Mackendrick and Lou Florimonte. Sandy was the Scottish-American film director behind such classics as *Sweet Smell of Success*, *The Ladykillers*, and *The Man in the White Suit*. All of Sandy's films are brilliant in story, staging, and aesthetics. All possess a sophisticated wit that was reflective of Sandy himself. He left the film industry to become the first Dean of CalArts' Film School, founded in 1970. Sandy had a hard exterior, but on the inside was a kind man who had our backs. He was in his late 70's, and still had the mental energy and vitality of a man in his prime, which he brought into every class he taught. He told us the story of how he left Hollywood after feeling heart palpitations driving to work one day—it had ceased to be fun for him. The opportunity to teach young aspiring directors and share lessons he had learned from his career was just the pursuit that excited him, and he spent the rest of his life doing just that. His story stuck with me because of how it informs Creativity: **Do what brings you joy.** If something ceases to make you happy, you must reassess why you are doing it.

The other leader of the Directing program at CalArts was Lou Florimonte, who had been Dean of the Theatre School. He was the Yin to Sandy's Yang, always approachable and willing to hear out any questions or concerns I had. Together, Sandy and Lou taught me how to find my story and present it in the most honest, authentic way on stage or screen. Both men were incredibly creative, but both felt uncomfortable with the label of artist. Sandy bristled at the term—he considered himself "a craftsman for hire." This ran counter to the prevailing attitude of most faculty and students at CalArts who identified as solo auteur artists. I don't think Sandy and Lou would deny they were creative—but they saw creativity as something that relied on collaboration with others—the actors and the many crew members who all contributed to the project. This made a big impression on me—the notion that **creativity is collaborative and is usually stronger when there is greater inclusivity of other people's ideas.**

Consequently, my classmates at CalArts became a very close-knit team; we all critiqued each other's stories and crewed each other's projects—we learned to be effective producers and had to be incredibly resourceful to get our projects off the ground, most of which were funded primarily on our own dime. We were in a hybrid program, which was part of both the Film and Theatre schools. Ironically, we were often treated as outsiders by the other students and faculty, who were protective of their turf, making us feel like we were not fully in either school. We had to be very diplomatic and persuasive to get anything done. Sandy would tell us, "If the front door is locked, try the back door or an open window to get in!" These were all creative producing skills that would help me infinitely later in my career.

CREATIVE DIPLOMACY

I had never been in charge of Craft Services before and was a little nervous. This entailed providing snacks and beverages for dozens on set for a large film shoot. After CalArts, I had signed up to be part of an agency that placed people into production assistant jobs for various projects. My rep called me with an offer to work on a Jaqueline Smith exercise video, and I jumped at the opportunity to meet one of the original "Charlie's Angels." I thought Craft Service wouldn't be much different from buying food for a party. Hardly. The job turned out to be one of the most hectic ever, although it was all worth it to have Jaqueline Smith smile and thank me personally for her smoothie. What my spread may have lacked in aesthetic, it excelled in abundance and variety. At the end of the shoot, the producer came over to the table. "I think you have a future in Craft Service," she said seriously. "The food may not have been the best, but you've got the looks to make it." I wanted to crawl under the table and contemplate what three years of film school had really prepared me for.

After getting my MFA at CalArts, I worked many odd jobs and went from feeling like a hot young director to a grunt starting at the bottom rung. It was a humbling experience to work as a PA, but also an education that I needed. I learned so many practical things—like what a production manager and unit producer do. I learned my way around all of LA county, going to various shoots and film and post-production facilities. While I met many amazing people in the community of crews, working production was exhausting. It's high energy and exciting but also demands extremely long and odd hours. It was hard to have any life outside of work. I began to long for the cool editing bays, where I could see the fruits of the production all come together in the editing process and where hours were more predictable. I got a lead on an assistant job for an entertainment advertising company and took it. I quickly moved up to editor, and soon after that, to "preditor," or producer-editor. I loved this role because I could set the pace and tone of a project. I also learned what footage was missing when I desperately needed a shot that wasn't there and had to find a creative solution, which proved to be a valuable lesson to carry with me to future film shoots.

Warner was a client, and I was assigned to a project of theirs called "The Buzz on DVD," which was intended to excite and inform A-Listers about this new format. It was a big success, which led to being offered a new position at Warner Home Video, producing creative behind-the-scenes content for films being released on DVD. At last, I got my Golden Ticket!

My years at Warner were filled with the unexpected, and while they included incredibly long hours, frustrating meetings, and constant scrutiny of budgets, I never lost sight of what a magical place it was. I started out as a department of one and, over the course of 23 years, built a team of 11. Together, we produced hundreds of hours of original content for all Warner films and TV shows being released on disc and digital. What I had learned about creativity up to then all came into play—it was collaborative and a process that included emotion and intellect, constant problem solving, and determination. I worked for a huge company with all sorts of protocols, legal restrictions, big personalities, and budgetary constraints. Still, at the end of the day, I had to make sure we delivered compelling content that told a great *story* and satisfied fans.

As a producer, I was a creative diplomat, bringing my Political Science training into play. I had to represent the needs of the company but also collaborate directly with top filmmakers and come out on the other side with something that everyone could be happy with. It was an exercise in creativity on countless levels.

I had many sublime interactions with the studio's top talent, with whom I had the privilege of working on various projects. It was a constant reminder that I was living the dream and loving it like I had experienced my first day working on "The Land of the Lost." I have my favorite memories—such as the many times I met with Oliver Stone while producing whatever extra content he wanted for his DVDs. He would wear slippers to studio meetings and always called me Gary because he thought I looked like Gary Oldman. While discussing an audio commentary project with Sandra Bullock during our walk to the recording studio, I noticed that every person we passed on the backlot was trying to appear nonchalant while actually staring at her. During an interview shoot for the *Gone With the Wind Special Edition*, Olivia de Haviland led my crew and I on a leisurely stroll across the backlot, as she generously gave us a vicarious glimpse into the Golden Age of Hollywood. I sat behind Barbra Streisand in her house, watching her get a mani-pedi while she recorded an audio commentary for *A Star is Born;* the manicurist, facing me and holding Barbra's foot, kept stopping to listen, mouth agape, fascinated by the stories Barbra was sharing. Meanwhile, Barbra's dog sat at her side and nibbled on chicken salad from a dainty plate. The morning after *Million Dollar Baby* swept up 7 Oscar wins, I directed an interview with Clint Eastwood and Hilary Swank, still basking in the afterglow of all-night Oscar festivities. I produced interviews with JK Rowling on multiple occasions in London, and once even with Harry Potter himself, Daniel Radcliffe. I felt like I was an honorary student at Hogwarts, only I was practicing movie magic. It was all part of a great creative collaboration that included many voices known and unknown to ensure the legacy of films and TV Series for the ages. That was a creative mission I was very proud to lead.

RESTORING CREATIVE VISION

The set looked beautiful—a gigantic backdrop of a starry moonlit sky hung against the wall, lit softly by an array of lights filtered by white scrims. My wife Jeudi stepped into place, radiant in a midnight-blue vintage dress, her moonstone necklace and jeweled fascinator shimmering in the lights. I adjusted the camera and began shooting the first take for the new music video for her recording of the classic song "Stardust." Just then, our dog Winston ran through the shot with a squeaking ball and barked at her, ready to play. This set wasn't on a soundstage – it was in our living room transformed into a studio, and we had a few unexpected interruptions by our kids and our Corgi to contend with. This is our wonderful new life.

After years of a stable job, my run at Warner unexpectedly ended in 2019 due to corporate consolidation. While I didn't choose to leave, deep down, I knew it was time. The last two years there were chaotic, with massive layoffs, budget cuts, and the disruption caused by emerging streaming services. I was spending more time in unnecessary meetings and less time working in a creative capacity. The job was losing its fun.

When I left, I planned to take some time to reassess my own goals and how I wanted to pivot. Then Covid-19 hit, and the shutdown changed everything. During those darkest days of the global pandemic, it was no surprise that people found solace in the arts; creativity both soothed and fueled our family, too. It was an opportunity to revive long-dormant creative ideas and dreams. I came to realize being freed from my job before the pandemic was a Godsend.

Suddenly afforded this gift of time, our whole family pivoted, and there was a creative renaissance in our household that raised our spirits and gave us renewed energy. Our sons adjusted to remote learning for college classes. Gustavo poured his focus into developing his artwork portfolio, often working through the night. Joaquin conducted at-home biology labs and helped me plant and tend our vegetable garden. My wife Jeudi is a singer of music from the Jazz Age to the Swinging Era, and in anticipation of the new roaring 20s, she recorded almost 30 songs before the pandemic roared in and shut things down. Now in lockdown, we became a creative team. I helped with licensing and distribution, and we collaborated on YouTube videos. I taught myself how to use the latest editing software to edit Jeudi's videos and many other projects. I remotely produce live-streamed Zoom shows with participants across the globe. I wrote daily, reviving a habit I abandoned long ago, and developed writing projects with colleagues. During this year, I was able to set my own creative sights, develop new skills, and prioritize what is truly important.

Working through adversity has taught me that the *unexpected* can be the catalyst of creativity. The unseen obstacle, the surprising thought that comes out of the blue, the hunch you get that is so crazy *it just might work*—all of these, when acted upon, can result in a positive, creative outcome. It is that creativity that has refocused my vision, opening my eyes to new possibilities for me and my family filled with exciting new chapters yet to be written.

ABOUT THE AUTHOR

PAUL HEMSTREET

Paul Hemstreet is an award-winning producer, director, and editor, with more than 25 years of experience working in the Entertainment business. During his tenure at Warner Bros. as SVP Creative Content, he and his team produced and pioneered over 3000 hours of behind-the-scenes documentaries and special features for films and TV series released on disc and digital, including the *Harry Potter* films, *The Matrix Trilogy*, DC Universe, *Friends*, *The Big Bang Theory*, and the great Warner Classics. An entrepreneur and innovator, Paul leverages his successful track record and business acumen as a producing partner at *Home and Yonder*, the family-owned multimedia company he co-founded. He earned his MFA in the Directing for Theatre, Video, and Cinema program at California Institute of the Arts and a BA in Political Science at Carleton College. Originating from Minnesota, Paul resides in Los Angeles, California.

Instagram: https://www.instagram.com/homeandyonderpaul/

Facebook: https://www.facebook.com/HomeAndYonder

LinkedIn: https://www.linkedin.com/in/paulhemstreet/

MUHNOO SOPHIA JAIN

COURAGE IS THE FIRE OF CREATIVITY

Fear has to be let go in order for creativity to flow; When we connect with the heart, Creativity is what we need to express what lies within!

*A*s the pile of my poetry lay there burning in a bonfire, I cringed at the very thought of knowing that some of my life's work was gone along with a ten-year marriage. I stood still, and then a memory surfaced. I recalled the first poem I wrote in the first grade. My first-grade teacher said she was very proud of me, and word traveled to my parents.

For the first time, I felt acknowledged—I felt pure joy for just writing what was in my heart without any 'outsiders' or adults telling me what, when, and how to speak.

See! I grew up in an era where children spoke and expressed themselves as they were told and had to meet the approval standards of the adults—or what is an appropriate way of thinking and the 'should or shouldn'ts' .

Prior to my encounter with the first-grade teacher, I barely spoke in my kindergarten class. I was comfortable staring out the window at the playground below my classroom while the teacher taught the class.

I would be mesmerized and enchanted by everything outside the window till I heard the teacher angrily call out my name. I would give her a blank stare and attempt to answer her question until my parents were called to discuss my staring out the window issue.

"Mrs. Jain, I am not sure why your daughter keeps staring out the window, but it has to stop."

It was my way of understanding the world around me, and people were less interesting to me at that age. I recall my mother getting nervous and saying to my father, "is there something wrong with our daughter? She just doesn't relate and is always in her own little world." Alas! My teacher sat me far away from the window.

We learned the poem about 'Rain, rain go away'.... but I never quite enjoyed it. I thought the rain was magical. I loved the way it sounded when the raindrops fell and hit the ground making a little puddle so I could splash in it. It was worth watching the rain, even if it made the teacher upset. When I got to first-grade, my teacher asked me why I liked staring out the window so much. Something prompted my courage and let go of the fear of what would follow if I answered truthfully. I meekly voiced that everyone tells me to pay attention to the boring things, but it is so beautiful when it rains, "Miss Chandni, do you think they are angels' tears?" And then I retreated and became quiet. My teacher encouraged me to write how I felt, which left me a bit confused.

Did an adult just ask me to write my thoughts? She did not get upset with me and call my parents? There isn't going to be a punishment for staring out the window? Instead, she embraced my quietness into a conversation to see what was going on in my (mental box). Whoa, that's strange!

Her paying attention to me inspired me to listen to my own thoughts and bring them to life for the first time. I wrote my first poem during recess and thus began my love to write and my first ever real friendship with another human being. Being able to express myself allowed me to start relating to those around me rather than being in a cocoon of isolation—the only way of being that I knew. My teacher shared the poem in the school magazine, where it allowed others to gain another perspective of the rain—of its beauty rather than the conventional thought of what was being taught.

About twelve years later, feeling unstoppable in my expression through poetry, I met a young man with whom I went ahead to have the perfect fairytale wedding that most people dream of. Like a princess, I rode away in a chariot only to discover later a prince 'Uncharming' and a 'Reverse Cinderella' who wouldn't be able to express her feelings through poetry again. Regular banters turned into a mockery of the poetry-

"What are these birds talking about? These metaphors! Don't you know how to use simple English?" and then I would hear laughter.

The last straw was when I wrote a poem to express my heart and a heartfelt plea for the relationship, which ended with him crumbling my poetry on the floor and then the rest going up in flames.

As the flames from the poetry warmed the cold evening that once was used to warm the hearts, tears rolled down my face. What all could I save? I scurried to save my life's work—my soul's expression. As I watched the bonfire turn to ashes and cooling down—ironically, the heavens rained, and I stood there staring at the demise of my expression and a relationship. I retreated into the womb of loneliness, where I felt safe. Days went by, and I longed for human connection.

It was a taste that I had acquired, and I had grown to love people. Poetry had become a way for me to share connections at a different level. It had

*allowed me to embrace and appreciate the unique perspectives we all had—
and underneath it all the same spirit we carried.*

Days followed, and I immersed myself in just observing nature—
mostly at the beach. For hours, I would stare at the waves coming in
and then going back out. It reminded me of the time I was in
Kindergarten—I would be still—no conversation, no movement, no
cellphone, no reading, no writing. I was like the bed of rocks by the
ocean sand that doesn't move but is there to witness the waves
coming in and leaving the shore- I did nothing. As a frequent beach
dweller, I began connecting to my inner being, realizing that I just
want to be. Within the stillness,

I began a different spiritual journey. I came to a realization that we
are creative beings and that without being able to express that
creativity, our souls are crying and dying. Rocks are often associated
with lack of emotion and no expression, but what was it that I was
feeling—it wasn't the feeling of numbness this time. Numbness had
been something I was familiar with—a feeling that holds all emotion
and expression and doesn't even know the mere existence of it. This
was different!

*Realization of a powerful being—I realized that expression allowed me to
stop being the bedrock who sits there emotionless and stoic by the shore, but
rather become part of a greater organic picture that is alive—the sand, the
air, the ocean, and the seagulls that stop by to rest a while. The stillness
that I felt at the ocean uncovered my spiritual being quite different and far
from being numb. Numbness blocks our soul from expressing, and stillness
is a holding environment that lets us choose our tool of creativity without
holding back, without self-judgment, and becomes part of the greater
picture. It becomes a gift we give to others and to ourselves because you
never know whose heart you will ever touch.*

One evening, I accepted a wine and paint invite from a friend in the
spirit of sisterhood. I disclosed to her that I had never painted on
canvas.

It will be laughable.

Maybe I'll just stick to wine drinking!

As I sat there with a glass of wine and a canvas listening to the step-by-step instructions, *I suddenly remembered about Meena.*

I met Meena in India, who was in 7th grade while I was attending the ninth grade. Meena was born without the ability to see and attended my school's integrative program in order to create a sense of normalcy and understanding for us regarding visual challenges. Meena and I would occasionally meet during lunch or exchange conversations in passing between classes. One day Meena handed me a card that she drew. It had a beautiful flower with different colors on it. To my curiosity, I asked Meena, how were you able to draw this since you have never seen a flower? She said, "because I have felt a flower before and I know you like flowers, so I made you this!" As I recall Meena, I am overcome with emotion in knowing that this was an expression of unconditional love- and that Meena drew a flower and expressed her heart to me through the eyes of her senses and touch. Someone who did not know what art is supposed to be like, what art looks like, or what this world even looks like expressed her compassion and love through her interpretation of what a flower may look like. **Expression is not about perfection or expectation- it is about authenticity and transparency.**

Meena found a creative way to draw a flower in her own way so she could express her thoughts and feelings in an unrestricted way. Creativity allowed her to break barriers in order to express herself. It must have taken immense inner strength to form her expression without feeling the need to 'fit in a box' of what her creation should be like and what parameters it must obey. Creativity does not obey, it forms its own path with immense courage to pave its own way. Just like my witnessing of my expression and life's work going up in flames- my journey transformed—I realized that indeed **Courage is the Fire of Creativity.** Creativity breathes life back into our spirits, so we don't have to just continue to exist and conform to the norms that keep us safe and hidden away.

As I completed my memory of Meena, I realized I had simultaneously completed my first piece of art on a canvas, and it wasn't half bad. Somehow, Meena's courage allowed me to break through my creative expression through art. This paved the way for me experimenting with art by myself—art in an abstract form that did not seem self-critical and self-loathing in nature—and thus began my journey of self-love. **Allowing creative expression birthed yet another milestone starter.** It led to me reconnecting to the world through photography. What caught my eye—a bird flying with its wings wide open I captured it on my camera. With every photograph I took, there was a story!

Fast forward into the present moment as I write this, I cannot help but bring the irony of life to light. Most people who know me as an adult, contrary to how I was in Kindergarten, know that I absolutely love to talk and express my feelings and thoughts through words. I have the stamina of 10 horses when it comes to speaking! **But all this changed suddenly one May morning** when I started feeling a loss of balance and, with it, the inability to form words and speak them.

I couldn't find simple words, and my speech became labored. I realized that I was still able to write some things down as to what I'm feeling and experiencing. I went to the emergency room, and I was seen by what has now become etched in my memory. I showed a phone-typed list of symptoms I had been experiencing, unable to speak much, and with a stutter, the doctor flailed his arms in the air and said, "why am I reading this? Why can't you just tell me?"

As he continued to talk fast, I felt a sense of numbness grow in my body, and his voice began to fade away slowly.

I saw his lips moving and his arms flailing

his body was just animating and spewing out words in an unfamiliar language. I could hear my own heart beat fast.

I held back my tears.

I wanted to scream.

I wanted to say, please slow down!

What did I do to deserve this!

But instead, I just sat there

MUTED...because the words didn't make it out.

My blank stares this time led me to being transferred to another hospital, followed by numerous tests. As I lay there with IV's sticking out both my arms with a fear of uncertainty, *I realized that not being able to express myself was making me feel oppressed, and my very definition of independence felt threatened.*

As I struggled to find words and keep track of what was being communicated by dozens of professionals, I came across a young doctor who kept insisting that I was probably experiencing depression and, therefore, unable to express myself. **I couldn't believe that it had come to this!** Deep down my soul, I knew something was wrong, but it was certainly not depression. I had had my experience with anxiety and depression in the past, and as a mental health professional, I took pride in my expertise. I was sure about the fact that I understood the parameters and symptoms of depression and that my true feelings are my own—and that I have to advocate for myself to the best of my ability.

The conversation went something like this:-

"Maybe you are very depressed and having a tough time, so you cannot express yourself." Not really! I enjoy my days and meditate daily. I usually love to talk.

"Maybe it's stress from work. What kind of work do you do?"

I'm a therapist.

"What kind of therapist?"

Mental health - Family therapist.

"Oh! That must be so stressful and difficult. I would get so stressed out! Do you even like your job?"

Of course I do! I've been doing it for about a decade. And I have a toolbox of stress busters that is bigger than most people I know! I don't carry the stress because I don't see it that way. "Well, you're a single mom, and you probably feel upset about not having much support." I have a great relationship and support from my friends, family, and coworkers. "Well, maybe the divorce had hit you hard."

It's been seven years since the separation and divorce, and I have resolved the pain and hurt. My ex-husband and I are now good co-parents. In fact, you may be able to catch him as he is going to be visiting and bringing my daughter soon.

I felt exhausted trying to explain what I was truly feeling—confused, annoyed, frustrated at the fact that someone was trying to convince me of what I must be feeling and experiencing and therefore having symptoms of something they couldn't resolve. I realized it's a slippery slope, and my laboured, stuttered speech wasn't really helping. I realized that if I didn't do something, I would actually end up very anxious and possibly on the road to depression. It was the last straw when I heard the young doctor say:

"Well, how about we give you this medication anyway. It's used for depression!"

Luckily, I remembered the lesson I learned from my first-grade teacher, what I found in the stillness of the rocks, the certainty of the waves always returning to the shore and what Meena's courage taught me. I remained composed and gently responded by explaining my awareness of the medication, its uses, and side effects if given to someone without depression.

After she left, I reflected on our conversation, and it took a few days to sink in what had really taken place. It dawned that as an adult who was struggling to express what I thought or

felt and as someone who is professionally aware of what depression and anxiety looks like, I felt so restricted

What must the people without this understanding and professional expertise go through, and how would it impact them in similar situations?

I realized that my journey allowed me to become more self-aware and creativity allowed me to reignite my soul.

The first rule in my profession is that we do not decide for others what people are feeling, rather help them discover it for themselves in a nurturing way. Whether it is through words or pictures or just an experience activity—the possibilities for self-discovery are endless.

Telling someone what to feel or what they must be feeling is robbing someone of the freedom of their unique experience. I think it's cruel— because it makes the other silent and further unexpressed. **When people with knowledge and power do that, it instills a lack of self-worth and strips away at it without us even realizing it.**

With passing days, I slowly regained my speech and my ability to hold conversations again. I recognized that not being able to express in the way I absolutely loved had been toruture—the very essence of my expression of love, encouragement, and power came from my word—the spoken word. The silence allowed me to listen to myself once again, and as I began to write-it formed an expression of my humility and a reminder of how sometimes we take the simplest of things for granted. It allowed me to truly understand the responsibility we carry when we hold power and knowledge- that it must be carefully used to foster confidence and strength and not oppression!

So many of us suffer from a loss of words when we are unable to express our love. Fear of rejection leads us to hide away when we are confronted by something uncomfortable. Being able to express ourselves allows us to be empowered and **Unmute** ourselves. Creativity is where we connect with ourselves and then expand that connection to others around us if we choose to. Our creative expression allows us to tap into our inner wealth- our worth and create value in not just our own lives but also that of others. It is not only a gift we give ourselves but also to others with a feeling of connectedness! **Creativity and spirituality go hand in hand.**

Creativity starts as a seed of thought and grows into a sense of being. It blossoms in its expression through whatever we want it to be! Through poetry, through love for people, through music, through laughter and joy from the silly jokes and art, dancing like nobody's watching, and through just connecting with the inner self as a spiritual being- an outlet where there lies no fear and a place where courage is born each step of the way- to connect to those around us.

Creativity is where I can experience that life matters- and at the heart of it all that all of us are creative beings!

- Muh-noo Sophia Jain

ABOUT THE AUTHOR

MUHNOO SOPHIA JAIN

Muhnoo Sophia Jain was born in India and moved to New Jersey at sixteen. Muhnoo's early work was published in the 'Teen Scene' for the Star Ledger, "Excelsior' Rutgers Preparatory school Magazine, 'Mosaic Literary Magazine' at Rutgers University, among others. She received the Outstanding Achievements Award in Poetry by the International Society of Poets in 2003. Muhnoo's life experiences humbled her to follow her passion and life's purpose in empowering others to recognize their value. She is currently working on building a community project in order to bring the feeling of 'sense of belonging' to group home youth. Muhnoo lives with her seven year old daughter who is also a budding writer.

Her coaching practice at Defining Moments Life Coaching LLC carries a unique vision.

To learn more, connect, or collaborate with Muhnoo:
LinkedIn: Manu Sophia Jain Kumar
Instagram: @Muhnoosophia
Facebook: Muhnoo Sophia Jain

DANETTE KUBANDA

CREATIVITY IS RESILIENCE

Cre-a-tiv-i-ty (kree-ey-tiv-i-tee)
Noun

1. Resilience
2. Solving problems in non-traditional and unexpected ways
3. Discovering new ways to look at challenges in work and family life.
4. A way to add emotion and magic to storytelling

MY DEFINITION

*C*reativity is Resilience. It's a problem-solving skill we use every day in our careers, relationships, and home life. Sure, we need creativity in art; that's non-negotiable and incredibly beautiful. But using creativity in the everyday challenges we face can add beauty into those would-be mundane moments we might take for granted.

A Vacation From Quarantine

My husband and I took our little family on a short beach getaway. After a full year of being safe at home together, we desperately needed a change of scenery. I was eager to build happy family memories, and selfishly, I was also hoping for some creative inspiration.

As I sat in the sand with my twins building a giant sand castle, complete with a moat, I noticed a tiny crab get swept up in the foam of a lapping wave a few feet away. When the water receded, the little guy jumped up and waddled as fast as he could towards the dry shore. Truthfully, the dry sand was only about 6 inches away. But, I'm sure, to his diminutive stature, it seemed more like miles away. Just as he was about to get to the dry sand, another wave swept in and washed him back out into the water. He'd paddle and waddle as quickly as his little appendages would let him. But it would happen again—just as he approached the dry sand, Swish! Back out to sea with him.

I felt bad for the little guy. It hurt my heart to see him struggle. But I'll admit I was nervous to help him. He had pinchers after all. I scooted over, sand shovel in hand, to where I'd be able to reach him. But to my surprise, when the next wave wafted ashore, my crab friend gave up and sank beneath the water. I swished the sand shovel through the wave and the sand below, looking for him. But he was gone.

I went back to my assigned job of digging the moat and immersed myself back into the construction work with my son and daughter. A moment later, about a foot from where I was sitting, I noticed the sand swirling around on its own. Then, pop! Out came the crab's tiny head, followed by the rest of his rough, crustaceous body. It turns out my buddy hadn't given up at all. He just creatively problem-solved a way out of his predicament. Now, I'm not a marine biologist, so I won't claim to know if a crab can consciously make the choice to find a way out of a problem or if his maneuver was pure animal instinct. But it did make me think differently about using creativity to solve a problem. I marveled at the little creature's resilience and wondered where he was off to next.

BACK TO (A NEW) REALITY

I thought a lot about this little crab on our 6-hour drive home from our beach vacation. I thought about his skill in using creativity to solve a problem and how I could take his lesson to heart in my own life.

As a TV producer, I've had to use creative problem solving in ways I would never have imagined. I've scrambled to replace a guest who missed a flight. I booked a last-minute guest directly from the studio audience when the scheduled guest sent her assistant instead of coming herself. I've had to charter a plane for a gorilla and secure a stretch Hummer for him because he wouldn't fit in a regular limousine. Working in TV often presented unique challenges that I can laugh about now.

I thrived in the stress-inducing, heart-attack-giving, anything-can-happen Live TV environment. But I also strived for excellence in the more focused, purposeful assignments of telling my guests' stories.

Producing and writing for TV shows requires me to use my creativity to craft compelling and inspiring stories based on my guests' lives: their hardships, their triumphs, their conflicts, and their transformative moments. It's a talent that gives me great pride. I have the opportunity to connect them with the viewers at home who are experiencing many of the same struggles, emotions, or questions in their own lives.

WRITING MY STORY

As I thought about the crab creating his own story – the waves weren't going to be the end of him! - I thought about how telling other people's stories on TV has allowed me to create my own amazing life story. And it's a story that I'm ecstatic to still be writing. Being in the middle of a great story is a wonderful place to be.

The funny thing is that when you're living the story, it can be easy to get caught up in the every day and not appreciate all the simple, wondrous moments happening all around you.

For some reason, that same creativity – the one I give so freely to my guests and clients in my work life – has been slightly more difficult to regularly tap into in my own life.

This has been especially true over the last year and so many months. We've been stuck in the house due to the Covid 19 pandemic, and creativity seemed like a distant old friend.

REUNITING WITH MY CREATIVE SELF

As a mom of 3 little ones, I watch a lot of animated movies. There's a scene in Disney's *Big Hero Six* where Tedashi is trying to help his little brother break out of a rut by bouncing him upside down over his shoulder. He says, "I'm not giving up on you. (Bounce, Bounce) Shake things up. (Spin, turn) Use that big brain of yours to think your way out. (Twist) Look for a new angle."

I'm not going to lie. I love this movie. Baymax is a big, inflatable cuddle bug, and the characters are so charming and really take care of each other emotionally while living their action/adventure dreams. But it's this scene between the two brothers that sticks with me in my day-to-day life. Tedashi's main message: change your perspective. I try to do that when my creativity is waning. Maybe I don't contort myself into some upside-down pretzel-shaped pose, but

I do try to look at things from a different angle & put myself in someone else's shoes.

CARDBOARD CITY

When my older boy loses his cool over something that seems trivial to me, I try to look at it through his eyes. One thing we've repeatedly clashed over is his love of hoarding cardboard boxes. Amazon delivery boxes, cereal boxes, all the excess packaging that toys come in these days: his room is often overrun with boxes.

His growing brain is overflowing with imagination. So, where I see a mess of an uncontrolled recycling plant, he sees a tiny city he's worked so hard to construct. To him, those boxes are the building components of a secret spy lair, a mad scientist's laboratory, or a superhero's underground hide-out.

The mom in me really struggles with the mess. But the last thing I want to do is stifle his imagination. By letting myself get into his world a little bit, I re-frame the way I see those boxes. They're not just garbage needing to go to the recycling bin; they are the stories he's building in his mind so that he can build the life that he wants to live.

Seeing his ingenuity through his proud eyes re-ignites my desire to create. And it has offered me countless ways to creatively play with my kids during all those months at home.

From paint gun wars to shaving cream battles to bagel art—one of our favorite lunches—we spent a lot of quarantine covered in messes. Creativity was survival for us. It kept us sane. It kept us smiling. And it kept us close. It brought out my family's resilience during a very uncertain time.

I've come to realize that I use creative problem solving in my new business too. I've always loved working in TV. It was a hugely rewarding way to use my creativity and make a big impact on the world and all the millions of viewers who watched my shows. But the toll the long hours and demanding nature of television production took on my creativity was something I had to consider when taking the next steps in my career, especially when I wanted to have a family at the same time.

THAT'S WHEN I FOUND THE LIST.

I have an old raggedy, ripped-out page of notebook paper in a cardboard photo box under my bed. It's a piece of paper that means a lot to me because it's where a 15-year-old me scribbled down a short list of life-long goals.

1. Marry Matthew Nelson
2. Have 5 kids, including twins
3. Work for Oprah
4. Win an Emmy
5. Travel and meet all kinds of people
6. Live in an old Victorian house with a turret room and wrap-around porch

I wrote that list while sitting in my girly teenager bedroom with its purple-flowered wallpaper and teeny-bopper posters all over the walls. I had crystal unicorn music boxes on the dresser and the frilliest dresses popping out of the closet. It's the place where I did my dreaming.

The very next year, at 16, I became a Boy Scout Explorer so that I could work at our local cable access channel. Our little group of five teens led by general manager Bill Phoenix covered city council meetings, local sporting events, and crewed community interest shows. That's where I launched my TV career. I wrote that list with a purpose, and I set out to make those wishes come true.

#1

Let's start at #1. Yes, I was captivated by the Nelson twins' beautiful long blonde hair and catchy lyrical riffs. And maybe that first entry on the list was a little too specific, coupled with a whole lot of wishful thinking. But people could say the same for my other entries on the list, too. Sadly for both Matthew and me, I met my husband PJ before our paths could cross. Ha! Fate stepped in and led me to where I needed to be at just the right moment.

#2

#2 on the list turned out to be way trickier than I had anticipated. As the youngest of 6 children and aunt to 15, including a great-niece and nephew, I naively thought having my own kids one day wouldn't be a problem. Unfortunately, after PJ and I were married, starting a family proved difficult, and we needed to turn to the most talented medical professionals to make our wish of having children come true.

While the statistics aim to make you feel less alone—1 in 8 couples experience infertility—the loss of such a significant dream can propel you into a desperation like no other.

I'm incredibly thankful for my husband's love, dedication and perseverance as we navigated a world so scary and foreign to both of us. He stayed strong when I couldn't. He continued to look for answers when I couldn't muster the courage to do anything other than cry.

And I'm eternally grateful for science and the gift of IVF. We maneuvered through anatomical complications, miscarriages, the loss of an embryo, and a vanishing twin before finally welcoming our three beautiful babies. I even managed to get the twins I wanted on my list!

It's hard to think of this dark, scary time in my life as a time of creativity. But we did continue to look for solutions, even when circumstances seemed dire. We were willing to try anything to fulfill this dream for both of us. And I think that's a big part of resilience. It's searching, researching, and continuing until you find a way. This is undoubtedly my proudest accomplishment. Goal #2, Check!

#3

When I was young, and someone asked me what I wanted to do when I grew up, I would always answer, "I'm going to work for Oprah." Growing up in a deteriorating steel town with very limited opportunities, I know many people thought that was a lofty aspiration. But I found a way. I knew good grades and asking "please" wouldn't be enough to land my dream job. So I started working for it. I looked for creative avenues to get me there.

I volunteered at Cablevision while I was still in high school. I learned the ropes of TV production, which bolstered my resume and helped me earn a scholarship to a Top 10 journalism school. I completed my internship for *Good Day, Cleveland,* a local morning talk show during my junior year of college, and became News Director of TV2, our student-run television station at Kent State University.

From there, I was able to jump straight into a job at CNN right out of college. And serendipitously, that led to landing a position at the *Oprah Winfrey Show* 3 years later. Goal #3, Check!

#4 AND #5

I knew if I wanted to achieve goal #4—winning an Emmy, I would have to leave *Oprah*. By the time I started at Harpo, Ms. Winfrey had already taken herself and the show out of the running for more awards, having already won so many. So, although working there was my "dream job," it wasn't meant to be my forever job.

After four years with the reigning Number 1 talk show, I branched out and started working on various shows for HGTV and Fine Living Network. These projects had me producing in the field, traveling the country, and meeting all kinds of new people. Goal #5, Check!

I loved the variety of stories I got to craft and create on my journeys. And even though I was traveling a lot, it was the most "normal" job I ever had in TV. I was able to enjoy a regular 10am to 6pm schedule when I was in the office, which was never something I had at any of my other TV jobs. I loved the producers, editors, and crew I was working alongside. But still, the coveted Emmy eluded me.

I took some time off to re-group and decide what was next for me. I nannied for Margie, one of my best friends, while she did her student teaching and bridged her TV career into her new career in education. These few months brought up a lot of questions for me. It was time to tap into my creative problem-solving to decide what was next for me.

NAPKIN THERAPY

I thrive during change. I get the most compliments when I'm off on a new adventure. And even though it may seem as though I jump into opportunities spontaneously, a lot of napkin therapy goes into them.

Napkin therapy is a decision-making tactic my friend Laura and I came up with while sitting in a booth eating cheese sticks one night after a late shift at CNN. We were both pondering our next moves and jotted down a pros/cons list on a napkin at a dark bar in the Virginia Highlands of Atlanta. It's a tradition that has seen us through job transitions, dating conundrums, and trans-Atlantic moves.

This round of Napkin Therapy found me leaning towards settling down and becoming a grown-up at the tender age of 33. I knew I wanted to find Mr. Right (whether he was Matthew Nelson or not) and have kids. But I still wanted that Emmy! So I set out to get it. Family life would have to wait just a little bit longer.

I accepted a three-month gig producing a court show in Texas. In July. I knew it was going to be hot. I'm not a fan of hot. I'm a fan of snow and ice skating and hot chocolate by the fire after a long day of skiing. But I figured I could do anything and live anywhere for three months.

A few weeks into my contract, I met my husband, and I stayed. Well, actually, I left in October. But then I came back. And then I stayed. This little 3-month gig turned into three years in Texas. I call it the longest three months of my life. But it gave me my husband, my dog Oscar and not one, but two Emmys! Goal #4, Check!

LIST COMPLETED. WELL, ALMOST.

It's weird when you realize you've actually achieved all the career goals you set out for yourself. And mine weren't chintzy goals. For a lot of people, my goals probably seemed pretty lofty and unattainable. But I was serious, and I looked at my goals with creativity and attacked them with a problem-solving mindset. I have great pride in knowing I accomplished everything I set out to do.

But it left me wondering, what's next?

I had the husband, and I wanted that family, but I knew I didn't want to be traveling so much and working TV production hours while trying to raise kids. I wanted to create a new career that capitalized on my experience and expertise but still allowed me the time to be the attentive mother I always envisioned I'd be.

A NEW BEGINNING

I created my own business and transitioned into becoming a media coach and publicity consultant. Now I help my clients, aspiring authors, experts, and business owners, become the compelling guests

I wanted to book for my TV shows. I get to be creative and come up with amazing show ideas while handing off the production work to other producers. It's the best of both worlds. I wake up excited to see what tomorrow holds.

#6

But still, that big old Victorian mansion eludes me. I haven't given up hope. I know she's out there somewhere. I just have to create a way to find her. Check mark, TBD.

ABOUT THE AUTHOR

DANETTE KUBANDA

Danette Kubanda is an Emmy award winning national television producer, writer, speaker, media coach, and publicity consultant. With the release of this book, she's excited to add Author to that list.

She's produced and booked guests for CNN, *The Oprah Winfrey Show*, HGTV, Fine Living Network, CBS, and Fox Twentieth Television.

After years of sifting through pitches from people seeking to secure a segment on one of her shows, she now is helping aspiring authors and experts fine-tune their pitches, presentation skills, and on-camera presence for the press. She continues to use her creativity in storytelling for both her clients and her on-air guests.

She currently lives in Tennessee with her husband PJ, their three young children, Cyrus and twins Ivan and Willa, and their Doberman Casper.

Website: www.DanetteKubanda.com
Facebook: https://www.facebook.com/DanetteKub
LinkedIn: https://www.linkedin.com/in/danettekubanda/
Instagram: https://www.instagram.com/kubandad/
Twitter: https://twitter.com/kubanda

MAYRA LEEN

BE OUT OF YOUR MIND: BOLDLY FOLLOW YOUR BLISS

SHE KNEW

I must have been only seven years old when my dad, who I only saw about once a year, was taking us back-to-school shopping. We only got new clothes during this time, so I knew it was my only chance for a whole year to pick the clothes I really wanted to wear. We were in a huge department store. I felt small beneath the midst of the rows of clothing and shelves. And that's when I saw *them*.

The shiny black books—they were perfect!

I shyly told my dad I wanted to try those on—I pointed. He said, "you don't want some sneakers?" He insisted I look at the sneakers and explained something about comfort and practicality. I did. I looked at the sneakers, and he said, "Which ones do you want?"

I pointed at the black boots.

Maybe it was the guilt of not really raising me, but he bought me the black boots. And for a whole school year, I wore the glossy black boots with the thick heel, and loved every second of it.

I also remember during this same school year wearing this silky hot pink shirt that opened at the belly button. I think it was originally my sister's top. I wore it all the time, even if it was wrinkly.

Funny how I knew what I wanted. I was a child. A child who liked shiny boots and silky hot pink tops when no one around me did. My mother always dressed very conservatively, and my older sister liked t-shirts and jeans. Apparently, I preferred a bit of glam.

SHE DOUBTED

Then, I grew up. I can remember time after time having teachers, my parents, and pastors make me feel wrong and bad for dressing the way I did. Once I entered college and especially Corporate America, I found myself questioning whether something made me look "slutty" or "cheap". Would people take me seriously? Was I too curvy? Was this outfit flattering? What message was I sending?

I know for sure that at age seven, none of those questions were relevant to me. I did not care or could even fathom trying to wrap my little mind on what someone else might be thinking about my clothes or what I liked. I was absolutely and fully tuned into my desires and my preferences.

When we are children, we draw, we create, we play. We do what feels good in the moment. If it doesn't feel good, we cry, we complain, and we throw temper tantrums.

But then, we're conditioned.

We're explained how to behave. We're told to sit right and act right, and eat right, and tolerate things. We are taught to let go of our intuitiveness in exchange for the opinions and advice of our parents, authority figures, and all the taller people in our lives.

What is evident to me now is that we are born into the earth with a full connection to the biggest, broadest, boldest version of ourselves. And then, we slowly or sometimes suddenly lose ourselves.

Unfortunately, for many of us, it was the only way to survive, to feel loved, and to be accepted. We did what we had to do.

THE CHECKLIST

We didn't have much money growing up: we always had food, but we never ate out, never went on a vacation, never shopped randomly, and the conversation was always about not having enough money or waiting for the next paycheck. My primary goal as an adult was to improve my family's financial situation. It's like an unwritten commandment in first-generation Mexican culture.

During my college years, I was so ingrained in my identity as a money-maker and business woman that I looked down on those who weren't as ambitious as me. How silly, I thought, to get a degree in art or social science.

It wasn't until I was 27 years old with a six-figure salary, three properties under my name, a fully stamped passport, a husband, and a big city lifestyle that I began to question my values and the purpose of life. I wasn't happy, and I couldn't figure out why.

I had it all—right?

All I *knew* was that I couldn't just keep going down the checklist anymore. What was next?

THE SUBCONSCIOUS

That is actually a question I'm still living with...

Because what I know now is that life doesn't have a checklist. It was never supposed to. Checklists are someone else's opinion of what you should do. And the only reason they ever gave their opinion was either to protect you from their own fears or to get

you to behave in a way that suited them.

For example, my parents wanted me to get a good job because they didn't want me to suffer financially the way they did. They wanted me to find stability and a steady paycheck. As a child, naturally, they told me to behave a certain way so that I would get along with others, so I wouldn't be so disruptive or considered ill-mannered by the other adults.

What I'm saying is that it's perfectly normal that we end up entering adulthood with a list of things we "should" and "shouldn't" do. It was installed in us from childhood by parents and people who had it installed in them, too. However, we must recognize that the intentions are based on fear—fear of failure, fear of rejection, and fear of the unknown.

Here's a couple of questions you can ask yourself to see if you're living under the checklist based on fear:

- Are you on autopilot simply living without knowing why you do what you do?
- Do you make decisions based on what would bring you the most joy or to avoid unknown consequences?
- What are you sacrificing for the sake of being responsible?

I began to unravel these questions when I started searching for my happiness. At the time, the only thing I could think to do was to restart the activities that I knew I really enjoyed: writing, reading, and working out. I immediately recognized that I had stopped doing these activities once I got married. I recognized an almost subconscious story that told me I have to be home all the time "attending" to my husband. The activities seemed self-consuming and isolating. Somehow, I had to be perpetually "available" for my partner.

Trust me, these were not conscious thoughts or decisions. I never considered myself a homemaker. I was a business woman after all, and my husband wasn't the type of person that demanded anything of me really, but obviously, that old traditional script of what a marriage looks like was there and I was blindly following it.

THE SURVIVAL BRAIN

We are tribal in nature. We want to fit in, we want to be accepted, and we want to be loved. The biggest trigger to our ancient survival brain is to be rejected. Avoiding rejection is a built-in survival mechanism that has been passed down for centuries. Those who survived stayed in their tribes by belonging, fitting in, and blending with the rest of the group. It was a life-and-death situation to defy the norm because if you were rejected and had to leave the tribe, you would absolutely die.

Now, here we are in a modern and connected world, still living with this ancient and limited brain. You can feel it in your nervous system when you try to ask for a raise when someone you care about ignores you when you feel judged by someone. It's so core to our being to want to get along and be liked. That's because to our brain, it's a matter of survival.

Consciously, though, we know there's no need to stay within our original tribe if we don't want to or if we do get rejected. In fact, there's an opportunity now to belong to as many tribes as you want and to hand-pick them.

You are literally able to design and create any life you want and surround yourself with people who will love you for it.

The only thing stopping any of us from the life of our dreams is this limited, survival brain. How do I know? Because if you didn't care to get along, and you didn't care about rejection, and you didn't care what anyone thought of you: you would absolutely be doing what you love.

OUR INTUITION

We have completely misunderstood the role of the mind. We live in a society that tells us to use our brain for everything: be rational, think logically. The worst part is that we try to make life decisions with our brain, too. But our mind was never meant to make decisions in the first place.

Say what? Yeah, your mind is a powerful analyzing mechanism, but it can't ever tell you your next step.

It doesn't have access to that information. It can only connect the dots looking back. It only knows what happened and can only project future situations with the limited information of the past. And it'll do it with the lens of survival as a priority. That's why change, new opportunities, and big decisions feel daunting.

One of the most shocking pieces of information I learned from one of my teachers, Marisa Peer, is that the mind's job is not to make you happy. It's to keep you alive. So anytime there's a decision to make, it'll point you to the safest and predictable route, even if it's miserable.

Your mind will prefer to be certain of misery than to take a leap into the possibility of joy.

And your mind is limited by the fact that it only knows what happened, and it cannot know what will happen. This is why your mind was never meant to make decisions. How could it? So, what are you supposed to do when you have a major life decision about your love life, your career, or your business?

It's tapping into your intuition, the sixth sense that simply knows. Greg Levoy explains in his book, Callings:

"There is power in trusting ourselves, relying on our intuitions, being able to act even in the face of uncertainty, rather than drone on for sometimes years with yes-no-yes-no-yes-no-yes-no, the very onomatopoeia of

indecision. It can be more heroic to be willing to act in the absence of certainty than to refuse to act without absolute certainty."

Another word for intuition might be soul, spirit, and source energy. In that context, all decisions become an act of faith, an activity outside of the mind, and absolutely an act of co-creation.

LIFE FORCE

For most of my life, I lived in my mind. I was my mind, and my mind was me. I didn't know any other part of me. It wasn't until I began my journey of seeking my happiness that I truly began to understand this soul aspect of me and began to pay attention to the signals in my body.

Finding your intuition, inner truth, inner guidance is key and possibly the only way to create a joyful life with purpose. You can call it god, but what I'm talking about is the unseen, the mystery of life itself. It's the energy that holds the cosmos together, the sun in perfect proximity to the earth and the moon in perfect alignment to earth and the oceans and tides in perfect rhythm, and the gravitational force in consistent power. It's the energy that makes a tiny seed into a giant tree and a microscopic cell into an entire human being.

This energy surrounds us, feeds us, clothes us, warms us, provides for us in abundance. It's what I would call the energy of creation. It's what started this whole thing we call existence and continues to propel evolution and growth in each fingernail, hair strand, and feather. It's constant and everywhere and expanding.

We plan our lives around the guarantee that the sun will come up tomorrow, and it'll do it at the exact cycle and speed and proximity that it did yesterday and the day before that. Despite constant motion and change, there's a consistency to the energy.

All this to say, there is this creative energy that exists in and throughout the universe. It's creative and cyclical in nature. It's in every single cell of your body, and it's the nature of who you are and what everything else is. You don't have to try to create, you are the creation, and with your consciousness, you are also an active participant in the co-creative experience.

Unlike the plant and the baby, which becomes what it's meant to be instinctively, there comes a point in your life where you become conscious enough to choose to flow with the expansion of life or to stop it. I think that's the experiment of life: to be able to choose whether to live in the understanding of this connection to all of life or to separate oneself from the source of constant growth and expansion. It's the choice to become the fullest, highest version of yourself or not.

THE PATH

How do we know what we're supposed to do? How do we know what we are to be?

That's like asking the apple seed how it knows to become an apple tree and not a rose. How does the microcell in a woman's womb know to become a baby and not a banana? Sounds silly, but when you look at the microscopic level of all that is, it's interesting that there's knowledge in a tiny spec. Doctors can stitch you up, but they can't explain how the cells know to rebuild your skin exactly in the place where you were cut. They can transfer a heart, but they can't orchestrate the blood cells to start pumping into it. The life energy is there and working for us. We're simply leveraging what already is.

So how can you know what you are meant to be and do? Well, it's ingrained in you, just like the knowledge of these cells. It's what's natural and fun and exciting and easy for you.

This statement is contrary to everything society has told you. We can't possibly do what's easy and fun. That's irresponsible, that's dangerous, that's absurd, that's lazy.

But look at the greatest of them all: the singers, the artists, the athletes, the innovators, the poets, the engineers, the public speakers - they love what they do. Looking from the outside in, it probably looks like a lot of hard work and effort.

Hard is what it would feel like if a bee was trying to be an ant. It would be a lot of hard work without much result. It would be burdensome, and the bee would die not only feeling burdened, exhausted, overwhelmed, disillusioned, and unhappy; but the rest of the world wouldn't have honey and flowers and all the beautiful things that bees bring us.

By not following your natural fun, gifts, and ease, you perform a disservice to yourself and the rest of the world. It's a piss-off to the universe who seeks expansion through you. It's a denial of the co-creative experience that is inherent within you.

CREATIVITY

Creativity is you being you—fully and completely without the burden of the checklist and the weight of the opinion of everyone else. Only you can know your calling. Only you know what feels good to you, and only you know when you're off track.

Your emotions are the built-in signals that you're facing the wrong direction. It's a constant, always available, always accurate system meant to guide you.

FINAL WORDS

I know life is hard. I know life brings us challenges. I know we all have our own screwed-up ideas and stories and dialogue that we adopted since childhood.

But I have a feeling that perhaps life was intentionally designed this way: A cycle of entering earth knowing exactly who you are and what you want and then forgetting just to journey back into remembering again.

It's sort of that up-and-down journey that makes the knowingness, the joy, and the flow a lot more exciting and precious.

I still have hard times and dark days. But I know everything in life is temporary. Everything is constantly changing, and every moment is new. I know that when I experience contrast, something I don't like, it helps me to see and experience what I do like with more fervor.

Whether you are currently in an ebb or a flow, I hope you remember it's temporary and savor it. I hope you acknowledge that you, beautiful soul, are part of all-that-is, and just like every single strand of grass is taken care of, every seed that desires to become a tree is supported, you and every desire in your heart are also heard and tended to.

I believe this creative energy is guiding us towards our fullest expression. Our job is to get out of our mind and follow it!

A Foreign Place by Mayra Leen
I had a dream
I was in a foreign country
I saw things
and animals
and activities

I didn't understand
I was confused
disturbed
and entertained

I saw my family
and my friends
and I aimlessly followed them

I never really knew where I was
or what was going to happen next It was constant chaos

I had moments when I knew I wanted something, but those around me
pulled me away
and explained why it was bad for me

I felt lost
everything was moving so fast
I just kept going
never really understanding where I was or why

I saw my spouse and my work
colleagues and when they were
upset about it all,
I realized I didn't want to be
I didn't want to follow anyone
anymore

As I tried to escape, I was mobbed by people having fun and playing with
fire I was afraid as they launched fire around me It felt out of control
They took what I had

I merely escaped and then found my items
That's when I noticed water and oil on
the ground
I dipped my feet and cleaned my soul and realized all is well

ABOUT THE AUTHOR

MAYRA LEEN

Mayra Leen is a certified hypnotherapist and founder of Be Out of Your Mind, a company with the mission to inspire more people to boldly follow their bliss by getting out of their rational, limiting, and survival mind and tap into their inner guidance, their heart, body, intuition, and emotions.

Mayra is a Latina from Mexican immigrant parents and former Fortune 500 Senior Manager with degrees from Baylor University and Northwestern University. She self-describes as a life enthusiast. She's an avid traveler, learner, and advocate for yoga and meditation.

Website: www.MayraLeen.com
Instagram: https://www.instagram.com/mayraleen/ (@mayraleen)
LinkedIn: http://www.linkedin.com/in/mayraleen/
Podcast: Be Out of Your Mind
Email: hello@mayraleen.com

EMILY NORTHEN

CREATIVITY IS... INTUITION IN ACTION

*I*t's 2012, and my intuition is shouting at me. It's been talking to me for quite some time now, telling me it's time to leave my job. I had been ignoring it, listing the reasons why I couldn't. Eventually it got so loud, saying if I stay in this job my health will suffer. I gave up the excuses, and I left the job. I had nothing to go to, my health was deteriorating. I was barely existing. I had no energy; my job took everything out of me.

But now I had time, I could think again.

And I had an idea.

I had always wanted to go to Italy to study the Italian language. I allowed myself to consider that idea, to wonder what it would look like if I went to Italy?

I stuck a pin in the map, Siena, googled language schools. There were three. One called out to me. That was it. I was going to Siena for three months to study at this language school - now the panic sets in. I have no income, and I'm going to a foreign country where I know no one.

A month later, I'm in Siena, standing outside the train station, wondering what on earth I have done. Nobody speaks English, I can't even say hello or thank you in Italian, yet it feels so right.

As a child I had always been considered creative. I was constantly making something, knitting, writing, sewing, imagining, dreaming. By 2012 I had not done anything creative for years.

But creativity isn't making.

Creativity is innovation, connection with our intuition, seeing the world with curiosity, interest, wonder, and I had lost that. I had lost all interest in everything around me. I was in this hamster wheel. I couldn't see a way off until I fell off and landed in Italy, where everything was different. Everywhere I turned, I saw something that inspired wonder, and I started taking photos of what I saw.

I learnt to live again. I learnt to live from a place of creativity. I learnt to speak Italian. It was a revelation to me. I was speaking Italian after just a few days, poorly, but I was doing it, and that gave me hope. Possibilities were available to me again, and I was open to ideas that I would never have contemplated before.

I stayed in Siena for three years, and I started to understand creativity — that it is a necessary skill that we are all born with.

Once we open ourselves to creativity and we allow ourselves to be curious, to dream, to wonder, to experiment with this one precious life, our creativity skyrockets, our intuition skyrockets. Opportunities that we would never have seen before land in front of us. And we say yes, what if I try this...

It is the questions that we ask ourselves that block or allow us to access our creativity.

Making is a way to access creativity, but *the two are not the same.* Making allows us to get into a flow state and is an easy way to access intuition.

Whether you express your creativity through making, your work, gardening, caring for your family, music or dance, or any other way, know that it is a power you can tap into any time; creativity is a power within you.

Creativity is intuition in action.

ABOUT THE AUTHOR

EMILY NORTHEN

Emily Northen can help you design and manifest a life that's in harmony with your Soul's purpose. For over 10 years Emily has been studying and applying transformational principles in her own life, recreating her own life and helping others build their dreams, accelerate their results and create richer, more fulfilling lives. Emily transformed her own life from one of illness and exhaustion to a life of purpose and joy. Her talent and passion for teaching and the power of creativity help you create a vision for your life and make it your reality. As a sought after coach, Emily offers inspiring workshops as well as transformational coaching programs that help clients achieve new heights of success, meaning, and spiritual aliveness.

Website: www.unlockyourcreativity.co.uk

Facebook: www.facebook.com/coachemilynorthen

Instagram: www.instagram.com/emily.northen

DAWN PHOENIX

CREATIVITY IS THE LANGUAGE OF THE SOUL

I spent most of my life believing I wasn't creative. I loved to write short stories and would spend hours just writing. But to me, if I wasn't making art, I wasn't creative. It wasn't until I was 43 that I FINALLY understood my creative genius.

"Whatever you birth is the way your soul expresses itself."

To me, creativity means to put something out in the world that wasn't there before. It doesn't matter what it looks, tastes, sounds, feels, or smells like. Whatever you birth is the way your soul expresses itself. Since we are all unique, there are oodles of ways for our souls to come through in the way that fits them best.

It turns out I create by receiving inspiration and information. I'm a walking, talking conduit taking in information 24/7. It's like I go through life with antennae perked up and always on. Sometimes I wake up in the morning with an idea for a workshop or program that has me tearing out of bed and bringing it into being before breakfast.

Other times, when I'm sitting in meditation, minding my own business, the Universe drops a download on me. It's like the Universe says, "There's this thing I want everyone to know, so how about you go tell them all about it?"

I will never forget in 2020, I was looking online for images for a project, and I heard the birds going crazy outside my living room. I went over to the huge picture window, and it looked like someone had put the birds and squirrels on fast forward. They were zipping around in an almost urgent way. There was this intense energy electrifying the area, and I could feel it, too.

After spending a few minutes watching the bizarre animal show outside my window, slack-jawed, I went back to my computer. And there it was: the image of a Phoenix I didn't remember being there before. All of a sudden, a message started coming through faster than I could write. It was the Phoenix Collective introducing themselves and sharing their story. I felt like I was in fast forward now! A few days later, I took their message and threw some images together with some music to create a video on my YouTube channel. It's still one of my most powerful channeled messages to this day.

A few months after that, I was meditating, and the Phoenix Collective dropped in a download that took me days to unpack. It was a 5 step process for transformation that they dictated very clearly. There was so much robust information there. I didn't have to change a thing to make it an effective tool. I trusted them to guide me in how to present it and beta-tested it with a small group a few weeks later. Everyone loved it!

These downloads and channeled messages are things that I would never have thought of on my own. The Universe creates through me, and it's always an exhilarating ride! I like to think we're all co-creating with the Universe to bring through our own perfect, unique gifts.

ABOUT THE AUTHOR

Dawn Phoenix is a Certified Clinical Hypnotherapist (C.C.H.t) and holds a Master of Teaching (M.T.). She is a Certified Dolphin Energy Healing Practitioner, Certified Animal Communicator, Channel, Phoenix Fire Transformation System Igniter, and #1 Best-Selling International Author. She combines these modalities under the title Transformational Healer.

Dawn works with people to help them release that which no longer serves them, reclaim their power as the true creators of their reality, and transform into who they were originally divinely designed to be.

Website:
https://www.dawnphoenix.net
Schedule a Session:
https://calendly.com/dawnphoenix
YouTube channel:
https://www.youtube.com/channel/UCerf61gAe2OY7eIQy5fJPTQ
My books on Amazon:
https://bit.ly/Dawnsbooks
Facebook:
https://www.facebook.com/dawnphoenixtransformationalhealer

ATOUSA RAISSYAN

CREATIVITY SAVED MY LIFE

I'm dedicating my chapter to two very special people in my life. The first is Ilya Rumi, my greatest teacher and son who always manages to amaze me. The second is Mohamed for support, encouragement, and always showing up. I am forever grateful for both of you, and I love you.

"*To be creative means to be in love with life. You can be creative only if you love life enough that you want to enhance its beauty, you want to bring a little more music to it, a little more poetry to it, a little more dance to it.*" ~Osho

How do you love life if you don't even love yourself? That has been my journey.

"Your task is not to seek for love, but merely to seek and find all the barriers within yourself that you have built against it." ~Rumi

The journey to loving myself fully and unconditionally began the year I was born, 1972, in Iran. I grew up in a culture and family where creativity was never encouraged, and the focus of life is being the best —richer, smarter, prettier, and most adored. Everything is about being more because you are never good enough as you are. Even creativity cannot escape the rule book. This type of environment is well suited for creating a life that is beautiful and dazzling on the outside and empty and unfulfilling on the inside.

Life, being our best teacher, will insist on our soul to shine, creating a radiant and fulfilling life. And to awaken you to your soul's intentions, life hands you intense training in the form of traumas and experiences. For me, this training came in the form of a broken family, an abusive father, Iran's Revolution, the Iran – Iraq war, growing up in a very male-dominated culture, moving to the US, and being in an abusive marriage that ended in divorce.

My parents divorced when I was two. My early childhood memories are that of a struggling single mom, financial hardship, and witnessing her emotional, mental and physical pain. Then there was my abusive father, who found his abuse as funny jokes. I was under the impression that he wanted a boy, and he got me, and since his first child, my sister, was a girl as well, he was pretty dissatisfied. Having a son in my culture is the ultimate achievement for the women birthing the child, giving their husband the ultimate gift, and for the man to be able to hold up his son that the family legacy shall continue. To put it into perspective, in most households, from the time the son is born, they call him "golden penis" signifying their importance in the family and society. My dad often would make fun of my body and the way I looked. When I was five, he told me I looked like a boy and that I had hairy legs and I should shave. Sometimes he would add a little torture to the mix. At age eight, he was drunk, and he grabbed my hand to force me to carry a cockroach because I was terrified of them. When he could not find one, he made me carry a dead one instead.

At age six, the Iranian revolution started, moving Iran from a monarchy or a theocracy. During the revolution, there were constant riots and gunshots. We were in a state of constant fear. I remember vividly one night, we awakened in the middle of the night to a sound of pounding on our door. A man was warning us to get out of the house, fearing the mob was about to burn the bank next door. We headed out running in the street in the middle of the night while looking back to see a big mob of men wearing all black, carrying torches, shouting, and chanting coming behind us.

At age eight was the start of the Iran—Iraq war, which I was in Iran for the first four years of it. And during the war, it was the constant sound of sirens letting us know to go to the basement or under tables to hide, and the sounds of shots and planes during the war and the big taped X on the windows to prevent breakage.

At this point, my dad worrying about his own well-being and future decided to move to the US via Germany. He figured his chances would be better if he took my sister and me along. However, after his second attempt for a visa had failed, he called my mom to come and get us in Germany since he was going to the US one way or another. My mom figured we were already in Germany, so best to have us stay until our paperwork was ready. At this time, I am 11 years old and get to experience racism for the first time. During that time, the Germans publicly displayed their hate for Turkish people, and we looked very similar to our geographic neighbors. After six months in Germany, at age 12, I finally arrived in the US, unable to speak a word of English, and during the Iran-US hostage crisis. You can use your imagination about the looks and words kids used and the difficulties of not being able to properly communicate as a teenager.

At age 13, I wanted to gain control over my life, and the only way I knew how was to get a good education to get a good job, become successful, and have money to gain control, love, and acceptance. And that is exactly what I did. I graduated high school at age 16, got my BS in Electrical Engineering at age 19, and got my first job as a female engineer. I was the youngest graduate at that time in the history of my college, and my father's comment when I graduated was, "so what, congratulations, now you can be a manager at McDonald's, who is going to hire you."

I went on to get my Master's Degree and made my first million at age 30—I lost it all between age 39-42 due to bad investments. This was the universe's way of bringing all my financial issues to my attention. As a kid, there was always a feeling of scarcity on both sides of the family due to generational financial loss and wars. Even if you gave my family millions, they would have an attitude of pauper toward money, but on the outside, it would be a different story. The attitude was that money is something that will be taken away or magically go away, so you need to save and always find a deal on everything. So, money is always leaving and hard to come by, and only a few selected will have a lot of it.

I got married to an abusive narcissist at age 32, had my son at age 36, and ugly divorce at age 39, which still plays out to this day in different ways. This was trauma on overdrive. Since I have a very high tolerance for pain, the universe answered by pilling up more pain than I could handle to get my attention so I would start to change my life. It's worth mentioning that the universe does this lovingly for us to release what is not aligned with the life we desire. My marriage was full of mental and emotional abuse, yelling, and breaking things. Some of the major events were: my ex threw a glass bowl at me, I was seven months pregnant at the time, and he barely missed my stomach; threatening me with a knife that he was going to mess me up; kicking me in the back after we notarized the separation paperwork; breaking in, after moving out, stealing my journals among other things; and later threatening me every chance he got that he was going to publish all my journals on social media.

During my life's journey, my body was trying to get my attention through a variety of physical ailments, some of which were: Migraines, Rheumatoid Arthritis, TMJ, candida, ovarian cysts, endometriosis, acid reflux, stomach ulcers, PMS, chronic fatigue, PTSD (marriage/divorce), anxiety, and skin issues. I worked out like a beast; I was doing CrossFit before CrossFit was a thing and could do two-finger pushups. My cardio of choice was running because it would make me numb. But, no matter how much I worked out and ran, it still didn't take away the pain inside. I felt unloved, unworthy, undeserving, unsafe, alone, and had so many fears and anxieties. The biggest one being that I will end up being old and alone with this very vivid image of me as an old bag lady pushing a cart in the street.

I spent my childhood and the first part of my adulthood trying to fit in and be loved. The message I was perceiving/receiving was that if I acted a certain way or looked a certain way, I would be loved and accepted. I had to be smart, pretty and skinny, good, obedient, conforming, successful, and follow the religious and society's values of being a "good" female. But, the cherry on top was that I would never be as good as or as powerful as a boy/man. Most of the choices and decisions I made in my life were so that I could be loved and accepted by my family, friends, and society, to feel safe and supported.

There is light at the end of the tunnel, and *it's how creativity saved my life*.

During the divorce, all the things my ex was doing, the stress of divorce, my own triggers, and having a very young child were so challenging that I could not work. I would sit in front of my computer to write design documents, but I was mentally, emotionally, intellectually unable to read anything or write any documents. It was as if everything was in a different language and that I could not formulate anything to be able to write it down. It's worth mentioning that before this, I was known for my fast turnaround for documentations and being one of the best employees no matter where I worked. After a few months of crying in front of my computer and battling this, I just stopped. I decided to take out my coloring pencils, pastels, and charcoals, that I had in the back of a small closet under the stairs and just started drawing whatever came to me. At the same time, I started reading Rumi again. This time reading Rumi was different. I was actually getting the real message. Then Rumi's poems became artworks with acrylic on canvas. It was amazing the more I read the poems, the more images were forming. I also started to do photography. Another form of creativity that I had enjoyed and loved but never allowed myself to do.

At some point, I was encouraged to put my artwork online, and in order to do that, I had to take photos of the art. In the process of putting the art online, I learned photoshop and lightroom, which opened my art to another whole beautiful world of possibilities. I soon began to create digital art, which made it easier for me to express what I was feeling and seeing. As I was creating my artwork, I received messages. Soon I was formulating my own words and poetry as inspirations for the artwork. A door had opened, the messages, like instruction manuals, were flowing to me, and each time I would get to see and release layers of myself. I had opened myself up to receiving, so the universe used everything to send me messages and guide me. I was using my 2004 training as a Master Energy Healer along with other tools that I was receiving and formulating to become aware of my layers, heal them and release them.

As more layers were being released, the lessons would become more challenging. The surface layers are easy to get to, but for where I wanted to go, I needed deeper dives, and the deeper you go, it becomes even tougher to see, heal, and release. It never crossed my mind to stop or change direction. As I was creating this new life by peeling back layers of myself, releasing and healing, I was also helping other friends to do the same. I got the encouragement I needed to open my own practice to help others. I was using the techniques I learned in healing myself for others, and now messages and lessons were coming in more clearly. My communication with my spirit guides, nature, and everything around me was much stronger and clearer. I also started getting messages about looking into shamanism. As soon as I found my shaman teacher, everything clicked. It was reassuring to see that what I had learned on my own and was practicing was what I was being taught. And working with my teacher allowed me to go much deeper into what I knew and was practicing already. Fast forward to today that I have a wonderful practice and have been blessed to be a part of so many people's journeys, guiding them to a more fulfilled life full of love.

There was a moment several years ago, during a meditation and one of my downloads, that I saw all the events in my life lineup and saw the wonderful map. The reason behind all those events and traumas, and the way they happened, was to bring me to this time and space. I remember being in awe and feeling an overwhelming amount of gratitude that no words could explain the feeling. I remembered I was very young and not even in school, watching the movies of different prophets, which made me want to be a healer and spiritual guide/teacher to help people. When you ask the universe for something, it gives it to you by showing you what needs to be released. My life needed to happen the way it did in order for me to learn all the tools and techniques, learn to let go of all my stuff, and relate and help all those that come to me. I teach what I practice myself in my daily life. Otherwise, I would not be a good teacher. And, I am willing to see my clients fully, love, and accept them fully, and I am not afraid to walk in their shadows and guide them to the light. That is why my clients have been so wonderful to call me a "Game Changer" and "Best Teacher and Mentor" because not only can I relate to their pain, but I can show them if I can do it, you can too. I guide them to release all that is holding them back, so they can fully love and accept themselves, trust themselves and the universes plan, and stand in their power. I have been blessed to be part of their life transformation, and each is a beautiful gift to me.

I stand today, more powerful than any other time in my life, yet humbled, and in awe of this wonderful creation we call life; I am fully and completely accepting of myself; I fully and completely love myself; I fully and completely trust the process, even if sometimes gets my body shaking and asks me to jump without a net; I fully trust myself and my knowing, I am worthy, I am connected to an infinite source of love, peace, joy, and abundance; I am loved, and I am love, I am creation in motion.

Creation in Motion:
You are made of the Four Elements,
Of Mother Earth and Father Sky.
You are miracle and magic,
a masterpiece;
you are creation in motion.
~ Atousa Raissyan

When you think of the four elements: air, fire, water, earth (metal, crystals, minerals, etc.), you can feel their presence on this planet that we call home. It is part of the very fabric of our existence on this planet. Now, connect with each one in your own body, air needed for our survival, lungs; fire is at the core of the planet and our core and needed for our grounding and passion for life; our bodies are made of 60% water, and the planet is 71% water; and the very fabric of this earth is running through our veins in the form of 102 minerals that make up our bodies, 99% of the mass of the human body is made up of the six elements that are the fabric of this planet. Do you think it's a coincidence?

Yes, we are made up of the four elements, and our mother is Mother Earth, our father is Father Sky. We are made up of the planet and the stars. If you are a child of the stars and planets and cosmos, how can you not be anything but a miracle and magic! How can you be anything but a beautiful masterpiece. You get to create life through this motion that is part of the planet, the cosmos, and just the very motion of existence, birth, death, and rebirth. We get to wake up each morning, reborn, with choices to create the life we desire. So create your life web.

Create Your Life Web:
You are the creator of your life

So be creative and patient
When building your life web.
Weave your dreams,
Add magic, add love,
Be gentle and grateful
Trust in your creation and the universe
For nothing is created without purpose.
~ Atousa Raissyan

This poem, which was inspiration for one of my digital artworks, from one of our amazing teachers, the spider. As you wake up each morning, let the spider remind you that you are being reborn and creating your life, so be creative, patient, grateful, gentle, and compassionate, create with love, and remind yourself that nothing in this wonderful magical amazing life is ever created without purpose.

Love and gratitude to all who have come and stayed, all who have left, all who are coming, and all who are leaving. Love and gratitude to all who played the villains in my life; without you, the lessons would not have been learned. Love and gratitude to everyone that has loved and supported me on this journey. And big love and gratitude to all my clients for allowing me to be a part of your creation.

THANK YOU

ABOUT THE AUTHOR

ATOUSA RAISSYAN

"Game changer", "intuitive, gifted healer", "guiding light", "life-changing", "magic" and "a blessing" are often how Atousa Raissyan's clients describe their experience with her. She is a Certified heart-centered Transformational Healer, Shaman, Spiritual Teacher, Digital Artist, Poet, and Motivational Speaker. Atousa has extensive experience in, and passion for, helping individuals to discover and tap into their "true self", in order to unlock their potential to experience their desired life, in terms of abundance, relationship, and personal well-being. She has been featured in Potomac Lifestyle Magazine, Entrepreneurs Herald, and USA Today. She is most proud of the positive impact she has made in her client's lives which is reflected in her client testimonials.

Websites:
www.atousaraissyan.com
www.soulystic.com
Instagram: @atousar and @soulystic
Facebook: @soulystic
Email: ar.soulystic@gmail.com

ELIZABETH SOSNER

CLOSET OF CURIOSITIES

CHILD OF LIGHTENING

$\mathcal{I}$n a tiny mill town in the rural mountains of Northern California, I was one of the 5th generation children to be born in the year 1969. There was a thunderstorm that August afternoon, and the only working car was an old pickup truck. My uncle drove with my laboring mother next to him. My father was in the passenger's seat. My mother recalled in her sleepy last days that every bump in the truck was miserable. The rain came in sheets, and they couldn't see the winding mountain road clearly. Lightning lit up the sky, and I came into this world just the same—light-filled and loud, she said. My parents were 15 and 16 when they had me. I was aptly named after a character in her favorite book. My rebellious mother, full of sorrow and insecurity, refused to give me up and was determined to prove the older parents and grandparents wrong in that she and my father could raise me.

SONGS OF THE 70S

My 16-year-old father worked the swing shift at the mill, went to high school before class to play chess with his art teacher, came home after school, went to bed, and began again that night. My mother dropped out. On the weekend, my hippie rebel parents were in a band. They would play local venues, met with groups in our living room to talk about protests and social justice. Tattered flags and Jimi Hendrix covered the dark paneled walls. When other children were playing Ring Around the Rosy, I was singing Smoke on the Water. Their best friend was my Godfather. He, a black man from another town, had to sneak in at night to visit. I would understand early on the idea of white privilege. I grieved the days I had to know what it cost him to visit me. He would be my rock throughout my life.

SAFE SPACES

Throughout my younger years, I sat in the company of 20 somethings and played while they experimented with drugs, listened to vinyl records, and planned protests. I watched while my genius parents with mental illnesses, youth, and two babies before 20, would fight and wreck the house. It was in these times that I would imagine my tiny house I would build. Wood-clad with my bedroom at the top of spiral stairs made of branches and knotty boards. Crooked but sturdy, it held me in its quiet limbs. My backyard trees held 2x4s in their branches. Each one designated a different room. Hours spent creating my quiet and peaceful home amongst the apples and bird nests. Cups and spoons, mud pies, and a tiny record player lived in those trees. I lived in those trees. It was safer there than in the house.

I learned to cook on an old wood stove as we could not afford the propane for the regular oven. I was featured once in the newspaper with my recipe for banana bread cooked in that antique stove. I dressed up my brother in my too-small dresses and mother's makeup. I would lead him around in choreographed dances to the Doobie

Brothers, much to the delight of my parents and their friends. My mother loved to tell the story of how I, at age 3, would put the back of my hand to my forehead, run across the living room, declare that I couldn't take it anymore, and collapse sobbing on the ground. The notion or belief that we are each other's mirrors could not have been more relevant than in this case of my mother and me—as was the idea that my dramatics were my way to getting attention. I lived in color. It was my home.

THERE ONCE WAS THIS PLACE

My father had a walk-in closet that was filled with things to write music, poetry, and create artwork. He designed woodworking projects and carved intricate chess pieces and walking staffs. He'd disappear for days on end into a closet of his creations before emerging hungry and finally tired enough to sleep. His mind. His mania. The beautiful curiosities are lost today, but I will never forget the amazing Papier Mache puppets he crafted from toilet paper tubes. I would tell him their stories, and he would write them down in his closet of tiny clear drawers labeled and filled with tools, trinkets, and guitar pics—a workbench at the back. There was just enough room for his guitar and a chair and a tiny amp. You could hear him scribbling lyrics and playing chords from his space in the tiny mining house. Born deaf in one ear, he would turn off his hearing aid so that he was completely alone in his closet of curiosities.

THEN THE DOOR CLOSED

In February of my 5th year, the day after Valentine's Day, I saw my father for the first time in months. It would also be my last. There is some debate about why my mother would not allow him to see my brother and me, but the general idea has something to do with child support. I was not overly eager to see him as I was too afraid to upset the temper of who it was I was living with. My 11-month-old brother cried. My father, distraught, left to return to where he was living at the time. Sometime in the middle of the night, we received the call that he had taken his own life. He had written a letter a few days prior that would change the course of my life. It was full of love, admiration for his daughter, and a request to "take care of your brother and your mommy for me. I love you all. I know I can count on you." Then he left me to do just that. A distraught 20-year-old mother, a little brother, and me, a 5-year-old who could roll joints, fix booboos, calm the beasts, and change a diaper. Later, my mother would tell me he was far too genius to deal with the real world. Creativity began to equal insanity in my impressionable mind. My imagination from this point would stay in its rightful place, and any creative endeavors I had felt sorrowfully impossible. After all, it must be palatable lest anyone think me crazy too. My imagination, my safe place, my home in color was not accessible for many years.

GETTING OUT

In the fall of 1987, after graduating high school, I moved to Arcata, CA., to begin my first semester at Humboldt State University. I had left behind a summer boyfriend. We had one pregnancy scare to which he was hoping it was positive. His desire was that I not leave to go to school, stay, and marry him. He was 24. I was 17. He was just a first step in my ongoing ability to pick unsupportive partners. Thank goodness, it was only a scare, and that my desire to get an education won. My dreams of being famous drove me to make better choices for myself. Dreams can do that.

It was at Humboldt State, I would find a whole bevy of incredibly imaginative, colorful, amazing soul connections. Only I was out of practice. I could not quite access what I knew was there somewhere hiding inside. I sat in awe of the others and their talent. Fighting for the ability to feel strong enough to share my ideas. Struggling to get through the emotional mud of defensiveness, creating often meant criticism. Teachings, I wasn't secure enough to hear. I discovered early in my life, however, that movement was the expression of my heart. For the first time, I understood that mime, dance, Feldenkrais, yoga, and strengthening my body gave me freedom and moments of elated happiness. I learned that creative expression did not always come with words or paintings. Stories are told with breath paired to movement. I was fearless when moving. I wore revealing clothing that accentuated my female form. I became embodied. The world began to move in all the ways in front of me, and I could speak the language.

CHOOSING INCONGRUENCIES

My boyfriend, who would later become my husband, found interest in a small-town girl as he was from the suburbs of Los Angeles. We met in the second month of my freshman year at HSU. He, a football player, and I, the nerdy theatre person. I was unrefined and fresh, and I knew how to pee in the woods. Unfortunately, I began to abandon my creative life in favor of spending time with him. Balance was not my strong point. He was dynamic in all ways. Loud and funny. It was also much easier than being with artsy people like me. It only served to remind me of my self-doubt. He came from what I felt was a fantasy. Suburbia Los Angeles and middle class. These things I had only dreamed of. My world began to feel not nearly as important as making a life of normalcy. He didn't argue, and we set off after graduation to a life of mediocrity. In suburbia. In Los Angeles. But what happens when two people not meant for that world try to settle there? In its most simplified explanation, you get lost.

TRUTH TELLING

Creativity showed up with my first job, teaching adults with disabilities a theater arts program developed by myself and my creative partner. We would be a team for years. Our close-knit group of actors were encouraged to learn all aspects of performing a show. Within its guidelines were the basics of learning social skills. We worked toward independent goals by self-advocating, writing, learning backstage skills, communication, public speaking, and collaborative projects. Their performances brought tears. Not because of the population but because they were raw, organic, and honest. We put our heart and soul into this troupe. They gave it back twofold. Creative freedom brings forth the truth. We saw growth in our clientele, but also in ourselves.

SEARCHING FOR FREEDOM

It was also keeping very well-appointed and decorated homes. Much like my father's little boxes of things, my life was labeled and appropriate. Freedom came from dancing in clubs late into the night and sneaking cigarettes. I would revisit this world again and again when the rebel side visited. I spent many hours rehearsing for shows, doing small commercials and films. A perfect excuse for an escape, I found my identity in being an actor. I created family after family with my theatre friends. Only to lose them once again when the show ended. But these people understood my untamed nature. They took me in with open arms and allowed me my bad habits. Shenanigans were had. These nights the process of telling stories to others became my savior. My husband threw himself into work and drinking. At our house, I continued to box myself in while he carried the weight of the world and lived without boundaries. We both suffered.

OH, BUT THE OPINIONS

Emotional dissonance is a strange thing. When two come from such different worlds, it often looks like gaslighting. His middle-class upbringing clashed greatly with my wild nature. My ideas were too far out there for the Stepford lifestyle, and my ideas and conversations were often turned back on me as if I had lost my mind. I was a hippie at heart, and that did not bode well for motherhood in the 90's Los Angeles. My children were allowed to sit on the table in their art room, they often didn't wear shoes, and they played in the street when it rained. As much as we tried to learn the flashcards, my nature was to raise the wildlings. Despite everyone's very loud protestations, both of my boys ended up homeschooled with me because, in all honesty, their natures were to be that as well. We spent every day thinking of what sounded like learning. We boogie boarded for PE. We sat and drew plants and identified them for biology. We found the pond with the tree frogs and attempted to count them. We'd buy old toasters and appliances, and they would take them apart and put things together again. They built a 6-foot trebuchet in the forest with an old weight set they'd found, soaked tennis balls in gasoline, and lit them on fire, provoking a call from the neighbor that she was a witness to flying fireballs from our property. We created every single day, and I felt as if for the first time in my adult life, my living color was being used to help these littles to learn who they were. They had labels given to them by doctors. Labels we used only to define strengths. "How would this be your asset?" I would ask. I wanted to be their everything.   How else could I show them unconditional love but to be a guide to their own curiosities and creativity. Their colors became mine and vice versa.

PHARMACEUTICALS

When we found ourselves in Northern California, the ghosts of my past caught up to me in a very real and tangible way. Finally, at some point after a trip to the Emergency Room, they discovered I had a serious condition called Non-Alcoholic Steatosis Hepatitis in addition to Hemochromatosis, a genetic mutation that causes your body to store too much iron, and a hypermobile condition that leaves my joints and connective tissues very weak. The liver was degenerating at a rate that was uncommon, and there was no answer from anyone. In 5 years, I had gone from a healthy liver to one that was 42 percent fat, 2nd degree fibrosis, and full of iron that indicates inflammation. The liver was three times its normal size. It has never been lost on me that the liver is the body's filter. What could I not clear in my body? It was here that I started a blog in an attempt to process this very serious day-to-day journey of confusion and fear. I found connection through this. I was named Liver Champion for the American Liver Foundation, and from here, I was hired to help pharmaceutical companies in training their lab staff. My story was a real-life case in which they could ask questions directly with a human they could relate to. I am still an advocate for new research in liver disease.

LESS IS MORE

About the same time as my diagnosis, I stepped back onto my yoga mat. I acquired my 200 hours certificate to teach. In addition, I added two more in teaching accessibly. Many people feel it is not for them due to the westernized view of what one needed to look like and move like in order to practice this ancient art and lifestyle. So, I answered the calling to bring functional movement to others who struggled with finding movement they feel safe to participate in. It is a daily discovery of new adaptations. The most exciting part is empowering others to find autonomy in their own bodies. To take part in community without feeling alienated. Each class is a new realization of how to address the whole person. It has been in this that I have found my people, my pack. Those that loved my too muchness, my taking up space, my heart in its clear little box labeled broken. It gifted me a beautiful group of women who are dedicated to doing deeply personal work that includes similar trappings as well as ancestral healing. It has revealed layers I thought not possible.

I still have my beautiful theatre family as well. As I changed, so did the relationships. They have continued even after shows closing. Acting has changed for me. I no longer look for identity in it. I find the process and the journey metaphorical for the character and as it relates to myself. At this age, the roles are different, and there is joy and freedom in feeling human. Less intimidating. Less perfectionism. Older theatre folk are a blessing. They tell the stories from a place of knowing. It feels less like acting and more like the giving and taking of an authentic relationship between audience and players. Less division. More symbiosis.

WHAT SPEAKS

The path we land in is one made up of all sorts of other people's luggage that requires unpacking. I was lost in the victim role for so many years. It was compounded when I became sick and diagnosed with C-PTSD. Tired of living this way, my creative nature and seeing life in color was bouncing inside of me, begging to find a way to speak. I learned to draw and to paint during the pandemic. I started with an art book that showed me how to draw women and faces. My girls that I painted were all the sides of me aching to be healthy. The soft, hurt, kind nature shows through in their eyes. They represent all of us. All the profiles of what may look broken reflect the beauty and strength we possess because of our experiences. The forgiveness in the blues, the strength in the red, our responsibility in yellows, the healing in green, and the peace and growth in the multi-colored flowers that surround them. They are not great works of art. But they speak to many in their imperfect lines and colors. I studied archetypes, read fairy tales with their hidden traps that I had chosen to walk into time and time again. I began to see my whole life unfold as if in a story itself. The players have come to this with a backstory. In order to heal, I had to release everyone from contractual obligations. They owed me nothing from this point forward. This healing was mine and mine only to have and to hold and to create.

OPEN THE DOOR

Creativity is where the soul meets the body in order to integrate and assimilate your reality. It looks like organizing your house, retelling of your day, raising your children, breathing with the waves as they roll in, and exhaling in its retreat. It is your story. In whatever way you choose to tell it. For every ending of a chapter, there is the beginning of the next. Death and rebirth and living in color in between. Rewilding it is called. It is that ancient way of bringing everyone home, and it's ours to create within our own closets of curiosities.

On August 4th, 2021 the small town of Greenville CA was burned completely in the Dixie Fire.
It destroyed the entire downtown and all the homes in the vicinity. The town was known as a
historical gold rush town and we all have grieved it's loss greatly.

ABOUT THE AUTHOR

ELIZABETH SOSNER

Elizabeth owns and operates Above the Curve Yoga which teaches individuals functional and recovery movement. This involves a combination of mindfulness, yoga asana, and myofascial release. Her goal is for everyone to feel in charge of their own healing ability.

Elizabeth is a mixed media artist who specializes in spiritual and healing figures of women. They are the embodiment of the women in her life that signify the perfect imperfection of those who despite difficulties in life, still approach the world with love and kindness.

Elizabeth is a hedge witch with a reverence for nature. She pretty much grows everything that can cure what ails you. She also is available for house and office blessings. She splits her time at her property in the foothills of the Sierra Nevada where she lives with her husband, adult children, 3 dogs, two kittens and the Sonoma Coast in the presence of ancient redwood trees.

Facebook: https://www.facebook.com/Beth.Sosner
Instagram: https://www.instagram.com/bestlifeoflizzie
https://www.instagram.com/madamee_artwork
Email: esosner@gmail.com

DR. KRISTINA TICKLER WELSOME

LIVING MY CREATIVE LIFE

*C*reativity is ... filling my one wild and precious life with all the whimsical fun my vivid mind can imagine.

Sunrise & sunset. Shared with somebody I love or enjoyed in solitary reflection. Over a delicious meal, I can savor ice cream melting on my tongue, a bottle of wine shared with a good friend, and some soul-nourishing conversation. Or eating alone while I relax and read an inspirational or entertaining book. Nights filled with music, fireflies, and dancing.

Creating success & surviving failure. Whether it's collaborating with others to make dreams come true or picking myself up and dusting myself off. Mustering my resilience and tenacity to learn from my past, taking the next necessary action step towards my future. Succeeding or Failing Fabulously but in a forward direction. Celebrating wins, big or small.

Loving the family I came from & the family I created. Learning to understand, accept and appreciate those who nurtured and supported me as a baby and ensured I grew into adulthood. The beautiful lives I've created out of love. Getting to know someone new, sharing stories, collaborating, and building a future. Saying goodbye and releasing old friends and relationships that no longer fit, suit or support me. Discovering and learning to love myself on the way.

New expansive adventures & pulling on a pair of worn blue jeans settling into old comfortable ways. Variety is the spice of life. Meeting new people, exploring unfamiliar places, and relishing novel experiences is the most creative way I know to live my life to the fullest while remaining grounded and true to my authentic self. Pursuing passions yet remaining present in the joy of each and every moment, knowing that pain and failure are the inevitable flip side where I will learn to become an even better version of myself.

Maintaining mental and physical wellness & challenging myself to grow and develop. Pushing beyond my comfort zone to rise above a new upper limit or taking a needed pause to reflect and feel the sun on my face as I peacefully let my mind wander along with the clouds in the sky above. Learning to balance challenging my body or mind to adapt and expand without pushing too far into overwhelm and shutdown. Sustaining a harmonic balance between all the facets of human life so I can feel holistically whole.

Integrating my divine masculine & feminine to create a safe and strong container to give my emotionally expressive side a safe space to come out to play and receive. Finding pleasure in every moment I live, whether the mundane and ordinary or during the surprising laughter that erupts when one of my children cracks a joke. Holding somebody I love as they cry with the deepest grief or celebrating one of their glorious wins. Simply being alone yet not lonely and loving and belonging to myself.

Creativity is leading a life that's open to serendipitous possibilities. It's expansive. It's colorful. It's magical. The universe guides and supports the realization of all my heart's desires.

ABOUT THE AUTHOR

DR. KRISTINA TICKLER WELSOME

Tina, AKA as Dr. Kristina Tickler Welsome, is a Doctor of Physical Therapy, Owner of The Key To Wellness and The Key Publishing, a Holistic Life Transformation Coach, and an International Bestselling Author. Decades of professional experience with patients, students, and clients, as well as her own personal life journey, make her coaching effective, efficient, and easily integrated into your life. Her passion is to support the well-being and healing of your heart, mind, body, and soul as you learn to love your authentic self. Tina will encourage and empower you to become the author of your own life story as you discover unconsidered possibilities, remove barriers to success and unlock your full potential to live a creative life you love.

Website: www.thekeytowellness.net
Facebook: Kristina Tickler Welsome
Facebook Page: Dr. Tina Welsome DPT
LinkedIn: Kristina Welsome
IG and IGTV: @thekeytowellness.tina
YouTube: The Key To Wellness Dr. Tina Welsome MSPT, DPT, OCS

WENDY VIGDOR-HESS

EMBODIED AWAKENING: BLOSSOMING INTO YOUR POTENTIAL

Dear One,

May you be open to receive the exquisiteness of your unique essence as you read, knowing you are not alone and are exactly where you need to be—creating in each moment.

---

*C*reativity births potential into reality through the unique expression animated within each human being. **Like a rosebud unfurling its petals and blossoming, we, too, become anew with the perfection of each moment.** From the beginning of our soul's journey, there is a unique, authentic expression that only we bring to this life. The creative force within animates our Beingness, so we give expression to the formless and blank canvas of our lives as Our Soul/Universe/God intends.

As human beings, we are meant to engage all of the creative senses: the _smell_ of the rose petals, the _sound_ of birdsong, and the _taste_ of a favorite food that makes our mouths water. We get to _feel_ a hug being held in love and bliss and have the ability to _see_ the magic in our daily lives through rainbows, sunsets, and loved ones that make our hearts melt. In our soul's journey of life, we learn and grow by interacting with our own environment and the connection to all things seen and unseen. Our body is one with Mother Earth, and when we realize we are Earth, making love to the elements of Nature, we make love with the essence of who we are. Through our experiences, we are being led back to remember who we are and why we are here, to love and accept ourselves as the Universe/God does, and to share our essence and vibration with the world.

CREATIVITY AS THE FRUIT OF OUR SOUL

Though we are taught to label things as good, bad, right, or wrong, what if they are just creative expressions of our soul, our Divine blueprint as was intended? All forms of creation are needed. They touch the collective for us to grow, expand and evolve, connecting us to the essence of life. The duality and polarity serve as gifts necessary for us to evolve.

We are like seeds—germinating, rooting, sprouting, budding, flowering, fruiting, and sowing, through an alchemical process with the natural environment. Engaging in our lives as creation, making love with nature, and honoring the cycles, we receive a more positive way to see or speak of ourselves and others. We can deepen our creativity by replacing and transforming judgement with acceptance, fear with love, impatience with patience, and stepping into deeper levels of compassion for ourselves and others.

Smile gratitude to your own heart now; breathe in acceptance.

GERMINATION: MY PERSONAL INSPIRATION

From a young age, I connected to what felt like a different world. As a sensitive, emotional empath and intuitive, I experienced the world through images, sensations, feelings, and sounds. I collected natural items for collages and often drew flowers and mandala-like patterns. I didn't realize until much later how these creations were guideposts that created a trail, like breadcrumbs, back to find the path toward my inner wisdom to share with and inspire others.

Being connected to a spiritual dimension and understanding, I often felt different, that I didn't belong, or something was inherently wrong with me. Hiding, striving for perfection, staying small, comparing, self-doubting, people pleasing, and seeing others as more valuable than myself were my secret friends in my self-created prison. Fear and feelings of not belonging held me captive.

Life was coupled with loneliness, staying busy, self-sabotage, and "doing distraction" in a variety of ways. I relied on my thoughts and though feeling deeply for others, often avoided or felt confused about my own feelings as if I might enter an abyss and never return. I spent years searching for "the thing" that would give me happiness or heal my confusion and illness. I went into debt along the way. I did heal a variety of conditions, including fibroids, Lyme disease, adrenal fatigue, Hashimoto's, heavy bleeding, imbalanced blood sugar, depression, anxiety, anemia, and Epstein Barr. After numerous trainings, classes, work, and life experiences, I was exhausted. I had become addicted to fixing myself, wanting to be heard and seen, yet running with distractions so I could not even see myself.

The insidious repetition pointed me to my underlying belief that I was missing something. It was a nudge toward a different direction than the one I had overturned many times before. Having accomplished a lot on the outside, my inner landscape was as dark as a dormant seed—where the flower and fruit are elusive, through a hidden and magical door. I realized that if I did not look in that direction, the flower would lie dormant in the seed. I could avoid this and continue to see more of the same or—awaken to a new journey, listen more to my "gut feelings," make a choice to embrace the hard work, and step into my divine spiritual self. Then I could have the awareness to...

Redefine and embrace blockages, struggles, and "darkness."

Have gratitude at the center for ALL that transpires.

See neutrality between labels of "dark/bad" and "light/good."

Trust that the "imperfect" is perfect.

Embody a deeper understanding of how loved we are without needing to do or prove anything.

Weave duality and unity in acceptance.

Receive a presence of safety where scared can transform to sacred.

ROOTING AND SPROUTING: CONNECTING EARTH AND HEAVEN

How does one "awaken the seed of our soul" and see that **we are sweetness, magic, and harmony?** We become one with each moment of expression, breaking through the illusions and stories and illuminating the Truth with ourselves.

Though I had an understanding from my intuition, believing, fully trusting, and embodying still eluded me. I had yet to allow the sun's rays to penetrate my shell and foster rooting and sprouting. Led by a passion and desire to unshackle and a willingness to be cracked open, I illuminated the dormant seed and surrendered to this deeper journey.

I learned to prioritize my life differently, to take deep breaths, and create time for stillness. Taking these actions helped me learn to listen to guidance from the universe. It helped me to anchor more deeply within my seed by asking questions about my discomforts and bringing them to Source to see my gifts in the sacred space of unification, rather than feel imprisoned in the discomfort and separation. When we feel big emotions, we bring acceptance into the heart, weaving heaven and earth with this presence of unification.

I was able to notice that my internal compass connected me to Source rather than to the mind I had come to rely on.

The more I listened, I literally danced new expressions into being, paying attention with a different focus. How could I embody through my senses to see, feel, hear, know things with more unwavering faith that I could expand anew through it ALL and play? By experimenting and playing more, it became easier to establish boundaries and space to have time to myself to engage more often in meditation, ritual, art, writing, and rest. I brought my presence to the moments, whether hugging a tree, toning a sound, stretching, sleeping outside, or talking with family or friends. When I learned to give myself pause to feel, this allowed clarity to stop saying yes when I meant no, even if it meant disappointing someone else. Simple things like sipping more water, walking, eating with presence, making altars, magic, and playing all contributed to **further releasing what I thought I knew in order to step more deeply into the unknown, where all creation is born.**

The days of feeling like a "bobblehead" with a huge dizzying mass on a small body were over. I could relax more into trust and feeling rather than stay numb.

Going from hiding and pleaser to play and pleasure helped me realize that no fixing is required, and we truly are not broken. Source always nudges us, and we may not always like what we experience. **The focus on fixing is a distraction from the Be-ing.**

Our creative paths differ in story, experiences, traumas, ancestral wounds, and the dictates of societal expectations. However, running from ourselves, thinking the answer lies outside of us, links us. **I am another you.**

We are meant to express our inner light to the outside world, yet we journey through a process of receiving kudos, energy, or approval from the outside world and label that the expression of self. We are programmed to look for love outside, emulate others, achieve abundance and success while often feeling jealous of others in order to claim our right to empowerment. We think we aren't enough, so we overdo. The desire for freedom, comfort, and peace sits there like sugar cookies with pretty designs, dazzling us with colored sprinkles. As a chocolate girl myself, I've creatively discovered new ways to add nourishing sweetness to my life and channeled my distractions to enjoy sweets in a balanced way (see SweetnessWithoutSugar.com).

Through this process of living, entering, and awakening the seed of our soul, we can re-write our story, experience it differently, and turn our traumas, awareness, and revelations into medicine that supports our unique vibrational frequency.

BUDDING: PATHWAYS FOR DISCOVERING THE FEMININE AND MASCULINE WITHIN

My work with women and families utilizes what I learned in awakening the "seed" while offering this reflection and possibility for all who choose it. In our busy lives, it is easy to lose focus on what really lights us up and instead succumb to tasks at hand, often with overwhelm. I learned to ask myself, "How can I take the time for the pleasures of life, breathe nature into my body, let the sun penetrate as I lay on the Earth, and make love to the richness and experience of life itself?" Whether doing dishes, laundry, chores, or carpool, it is possible to open up to magic in the mundane, connecting to the creative force and possibilities not yet seen. It lights me up to help women redefine priorities putting their pleasure and self-care "on the list." **This sacred act IS the anchoring of the seed that then germinates and spreads wildflowers of beauty for all who surround her to behold.**

As a foundation, this work connects with the essence of a triangle, flower, and circle. The triangle often signifies growth-filled cycles leading to changed ways of being. Throughout time, we speak of creation in 3's such as past, present, future, or mother, father, and child. These can signify the three points of the triangle which is woven into the very fibers of our existence.

We are stepping into the divine feminine and divine masculine as energetic forces, both of which have been wounded in a patriarchal culture. **During this time of great change in our world, we are awakening to the opportunity to navigate anew, leading from *balanced* divine feminine and divine masculine forces within.** A new beginning is unfolding, opening to the unification of heaven and earth, returning the codes that have patiently waited for this time where each person recognizes their wholeness, their sense of belonging, self-love, unity, harmony, and acceptance. Children being born now understand this love language and often point those who are parents in this direction. They are the beacons of light teaching their parents to open their eyes and ears to listen, feel and see through the eyes of the heart, the natural environment, and a divine order that is shifting on the planet through all we are going through now.

Even amidst great polarity, we resonate with these truths like the light creating rays through the forest canopy.

Together, the process holds sacred, an awakening to a new belonging encircled with support. The more congruent we are in our truth, the more harmony, play, and radiance ripples forth.

As the process of uncovering one's unique signature and expression unfolds, we embark on a creative process with a canvas of our own making. What makes a person? Why is that person here? What is their purpose, and how are they meant to express that? As an intuitive guide, healer, and coach, how can I guide them in teasing apart what their truth is from what they were conditioned to think was their creative expression?

Utilizing different modalities and tapping into conscious and unconscious realms, my work guides women and families to learn to separate out who they are versus all that was collected, like a sponge, from the world around them. The process gives permission for a person to squeeze the sponge so that all that remains go back to the empty canvas, releasing what no longer serves or what was never theirs. We are free to honor our past with gratitude and embrace where we are going.

FLOWERING: INTEGRATION AND UNITY

Just as a growing sprout organically flowers with enough sunlight, nutrients, and connection to the elements, we have the opportunity to follow our rhythms and fully embody our potential. We learn, remember, and return to listen deeply to the pulse of the universe and our own pulse, to what is needed for us, our families, and the planet. As a baby hears the sounds and feels all of the feels, they may jump at the sound of a lawn mower but not at the birds outside. All of their senses are engaged—vision, hearing, seeing, smelling, tasting. How do we envelop ourselves in all of this creation and receive the reflection to us? By walking barefoot to feel the earth beneath our feet and to drink in all that it gives, we can tap into the crystalline core, the minerals of the earth, the slower pace, and vitality.

Though a container exists in this multi-petaled approach, potential and the formless becomes form as created by the individual. Honoring the parts that have been forgotten and expressing the fullness of oneself opens the authentic self to be seen and felt.

Together, we move towards this reconnection. Beginning with the individual, shifting limiting beliefs, pains, and struggles, messages ingrained or modeled for us, we befriend the lessons and the bigger picture, bringing acceptance to all of this. We learn to see with forgiveness, gratitude, and more clarity that all of it has happened being part of this living structure. Each person goes through this in their own way. Why compare when in tune with this creative force, we all follow our own timing? This encourages us to open our eyes to see more clearly and to embrace the essence and core of who we are, who we are born to be, and who we are awakening to become.

FRUITING: FAMILY AS A PORTAL TO BROADEN CONNECTIONS

Just as nature is a rhythmic moving system, the families of the world reflect this connection because we are nature itself. Nature is never stagnant or quiet, yet there is stillness. Like the apples that fall from the tree are used to feed animals or provide nutrients for the soil and new sprouting seeds; hence, nothing is lost. Through the release from the tree, there is rebirth and renewal. Similarly, through the shifts and changes in families, the rhythms become embodied anew.

As individuals and families begin to reconnect to their natural rhythms and give attention to the feelings that weren't expressed or couldn't be, the paradigm can shift. This awakening helps open to joy, to what has been searched for from outside oneself. Yet, like the seed, it's all inside. It is available to all and yet unique to each person's frequency to remember who they are so they can express that from their own understanding. Children demonstrate this through their innate understanding of their language. One of our daughter's favorite expressions was "Why Can Do?" Wanting to know why, expressing enthusiasm for living life to the fullest as an adventurous spirit here to question and be an agent for change. Our son said, "Take a bang at it," to step in and try, willing to experience new things and take the simple act of playing.

Choosing connection, compassion, and support yields a more plentiful harvest for all.

SOWING SOURCE: BLOSSOMING INTO WHO YOU REALLY ARE

The time is here for those who choose to step into the path of awakening, choose love over fear, dissolve and surrender what we thought we knew into what we are envisioning for a bright future. By listening to Source, healing our partnership wounds, creating sovereign and true support of ourselves and others, we liberate the wounds of our past and ancestral trauma. We step out of hiding, automatic pilot and shut down and surrender to Let Love Lead by making love every day in the simplest ways.

To teach self-love, we must be self-love. In the demonstration, kids learn, modeling some of what we do and following their own impulses, having little or nothing to do with us as they come through us yet belong to the Universe and their own sovereign selves. These resilient children will be leading the generations to come.

As parents and partners (single, together, or not), the more we heal our past and step into our self-mastery and radiance, the more this portal expands for our kids to enter, allowing them to be different from us and to encourage their fullest expression.

What results elevates each person to open and blossom into their pleasure and joy, which then spreads. When each person is singing their unique signature, it creates more vibrations of love and oneness. The planet as a living unit grows and expands in harmony.

Having suffered in my own self-imposed prison, I love to help illuminate the creation that is possible for each soul, pointing you inside to connect with the compass that has always been there: your flower, mandala, and vision. Awaken to the possibility of taking all you have learned, using the magic inside of you and through the Universe/Source to create the life you want. I invite you to step in and Trust the alchemical process that will unfold. The depth of love in the duality and the dance of magic is a creation worth embodying.

As we shift our compass to Source, we, as Divine Creators, can together awaken to the forces of nature, beingness, and consciousness. This can ultimately allow us to bloom and connect to Creating—Whatever We Want to Be!

I welcome you to walk in community with me. Go to this link to listen to this meditation www.vigdorhess.com/leading-with-love

May you give yourself permission to
"Release the Do and Just Be You for a Self-Loved, Soul-Led Life!"
Sending you love and blessings,
Wendy

ABOUT THE AUTHOR
WENDY VIGDOR-HESS

Wendy Vigdor-Hess is a visionary, guide, and coach specializing in helping people awaken, reconnect with themselves and a greater Source to lead their lives and families with love, freedom, ease, empowerment, and purpose. As an intuitive empathic healer, shaman, registered dietitian, author, speaker, and guide, she supports people to listen more deeply to their inner voice and embrace the alchemy from chaos to calm.

People benefit from Wendy's unique multi-petaled approach, by becoming who they want to be, bridging the gap from looking outside oneself to receiving the sweetness of their gifts within. Her podcast and other interviews demonstrate her passion and positive energy exchange with others inspiring transformation, connection, self-love and acceptance.

Wendy loves time with her husband, kids and animals. She enjoys communing with nature, walking barefoot, dancing, hiking, ritual, magic, yoga, travel and connection with family and friends.

Website: www.vigdorhess.com
Email: wendy@vigdorhess.com
Facebook: www.facebook.com/wendyvigdorhess
Facebook Group for Women and Moms: https://www.facebook.com/groups/1021610851652778
Instagram: wendyvigdorhess

ABOUT THE PUBLISHER

Express Yourself
PUBLISHING

*H*ollis Citron is on a mission to expand the definition of creativity beyond a pencil and a paintbrush. She is the founder of Express Yourself Publishing, founder and CEO of I Am Creative and a podcast host of Creative Conversations with Hollis Citron.

She has been an art teacher for 25+ years working with children and adults with all different abilities and is all about empowering individuals to express themselves in whatever format that looks like for them and to be exposed to new possibilities. She is here to fight for the inner voice in your head that screams every time someone tells you that you and your creative expression is less than. She is here to fight for your ability to explore your creative story, we all have one!

Hollis believes that there is power in the written word and people sharing their stories create connections. When people see themselves as creators and creatives they feel purposeful and are at their core happy

Let's show them how together if we learn to open our minds and our thoughts, that we can change the world.

Yes, you ARE creative. And don't let anyone tell you otherwise.

Printed in Great Britain
by Amazon

21114946R00112